YOUR GIANTS ARE LYING TO YOU

THE TRUTH ABOUT FEAR, FAILURE, AND FINDING YOURSELF

RYAN FINKLE

© 2025 RYAN FINKLE

All rights reserved. No portion of this book may be reproduced, copied, distributed or adapted in any way, except for certain activities permitted by applicable copyright laws, such as brief quotations in context of a review or article. For permission to publish, distribute or otherwise reproduce this work, please contact the author.

Scriptures taken from the New King James Version®.
Copyright © 1982 by Thomas Nelson. Used by permission. All rights reserved.

CONTENTS

INTRODUCTION 7

1. THE FEAR-DRIVEN ACHIEVER: A LIFE DEFINED BY PROVING 13
   DOUBLING DOWN IN UNIFORM 35
2. THE INJURY THAT CHANGED EVERYTHING 37
3. JACOB'S WRESTLE: FIGHTING FOR IDENTITY 53
4. WALKING WITH A LIMP 79
5. FACING GOLIATH - FEAR, COURAGE, AND DESTINY COLLIDE 101
6. WHEN THE CALLING BURNS: PURPOSE REMAINS 121
7. LEADING WHILE LIMPING: REDEFINING STRENGTH IN LEADERSHIP 135
8. WRESTLING, LIMPING, WINNING—REFRAMING THE PAST 149
9. WALKING INTO PURPOSE: LIVING WITH A NEW IDENTITY 165
10. THE RIPPLE EFFECT - WHEN YOU MULTIPLY THE SHIFT 177
    THIS IS THE MOMENT 198
    WANT TO GO DEEPER? 200
    ABOUT RYAN 202

INTRODUCTION

*"Our greatest fear should not be of failure,
but of succeeding at something that doesn't really matter."*
— **D.L. Moody** (1837-1899), American evangelist & educator

For most of my life, I focused on the second half of that quote. I didn't want to waste my life. I didn't want to chase something hollow. I wanted to succeed at something that really mattered.

So I set out to do exactly that—chase meaning, build legacy, live with purpose. But I never stopped to examine the first part of Moody's quote: **"Our greatest fear…"**

Looking back now, I see it clearly.
I wasn't just driven by purpose.
I was driven by fear.
Fear of being ordinary.
Fear of being left behind.
Fear of not doing enough.
Fear of failure—dressed up to look like ambition.

And when you're fear-driven, you don't slow down.
You double down.
That's exactly what I did.
I didn't ask, *"What's the right path?"*
I asked, *"What's the path that proves I belong?"*

Not long after graduating college—on the tail end of the 2008 financial crisis—I enlisted in the U.S. Army Reserve. Both of my brothers had joined the National Guard, and their paths stirred something in me. I came across the Civil Affairs Specialist role—humanitarian, strategic, deeply needed. It spoke to me. Helping others. Building stability. Creating change. It felt like calling. But underneath the surface, something else was happening.

I didn't see a clear way forward. I felt like I was falling behind. I couldn't afford to fail. So I picked the hardest, most respectable path I could find—and I doubled down.

Enlisting wasn't just a decision. It was a statement. To the world. To myself. **"See? I'm doing something that really matters."** But I didn't yet know the cost.

What fear-driven achievement never tells you is this: eventually, fear catches up. And when it does, it doesn't tap you on the shoulder—it takes something. Your health. Your clarity. Your voice. And ultimately, your identity—the real you.

INTRODUCTION

For me, it took my hip.

A basic training injury marked the beginning of a years-long journey—through physical pain, internal collapse, disorientation, and eventually, healing.

Not just in body.

In soul.

And along the way, I learned something else:

The giants you think are standing in your way?

They're often lying to you.
They lie about your worth.
They lie about what success should look like.
They lie about how far you still have to go before you're "enough."

They lie about your identity.

But if you're willing to stop performing long enough to listen—to slow down. To wrestle. To ask better questions—You'll find something waiting on the other side of fear.

You.

Not the version of you built to impress.
Not the version of you trained to survive.
But the version of you that was there all along—

Strong.
Grounded.
Purposeful.

That's what this book is about. It's not about how to conquer giants. It's about how to stop believing them.

Because the lies they tell?
They often sound like truth.

INTRODUCTION

Before We Begin...

This book is for you if...
You've already succeeded at a few things in life.
You've made decisions, led people, hit goals, and kept moving.
But quietly—maybe even unknowingly—you carry the weight of your own success.

You feel pressure to deliver, even when no one's asking.
You over-prepare because you're afraid of missing something important. You've built trust by being strong—even when you feel unsteady inside.

You crave rest but don't know how to stop without guilt. You're constantly measuring—expectations, outcomes, reactions. You've learned to function under pressure, and you're excellent at it. But part of you is starting to wonder... *"Can I really keep this up?"* You don't feel like an imposter. But you're not fully convinced you belong, either.

Completion doesn't come from applause.
It comes from relief.
From rest.
From truth.

If any of that sounds familiar—you're not alone. You're not broken. You're not behind. You're just standing at the edge of something deeper. A quieter kind of courage. The kind that doesn't prove anything—but finally tells the truth. This is your invitation. To move from driven to grounded. From fearful to faithful. From striving to whole. That's what freedom from fear looks like.

Let's begin the real work. The internal kind.

You don't need to chase a better version of you.
You just need to come home to the true one –
the self fear tried to hide and grace keeps calling back.

What story have you been telling yourself about what makes you worthy?

Chapter 1

THE FEAR-DRIVEN ACHIEVER: A LIFE DEFINED BY PROVING

I didn't always know I was afraid.
I just knew I couldn't afford to get it wrong.

It was junior high—marching band season, Friday night under the lights. The cafeteria was dim except for the flickering lights of a DJ booth in the corner. That's when it happened.

We had just come off the football field, me with my French horn, sweating and proud. Back in the bleachers, she walked over. Someone I liked. Not a passing crush—the real kind. The kind where your pulse races for reasons you don't fully understand.

She smiled—bold, disarming—and asked if I wanted to go to the school dance the next week. I panicked, but tried to play it cool. "I'll have to ask my parents," I told her. She didn't wait. She jogged up the bleachers and asked for me. My parents both said yes. It was settled.

That should have been my moment. But when the night came, and the music swelled under those cafeteria lights, she found me again—still smiling, still kind, still hoping.

"Want to dance this one?" she asked.
I smiled and said, "Maybe the next one."
But the next one never came.

The truth? I didn't freeze because I didn't want to dance. I froze because I didn't want to fail. I didn't know how to dance. I was afraid I'd look foolish. Afraid she'd change her mind once she saw the real me. Afraid I'd embarrass her.

So I stood still, composed, while the music played. And I told myself it wasn't a big deal. That she probably asked everyone. That maybe it didn't mean what I thought it meant. But I knew. Even then—I knew. And now, 25 years later, I can finally name it:

That wasn't just a missed dance – that was the first echo of a story fear would keep repeating.

Fear doesn't always show up like a fire alarm. It doesn't scream. It whispers. "Don't risk it." That whisper keeps you off the dance floor. Out of the spotlight. Behind a carefully curated image—for years.

I was already being named by fear. Not with words, but with choices. In how I moved. How I stayed small. How I wore "quiet" like a badge—because it felt safer than being fully seen. Safer than being playful. Safer than having fun.

I had already started preserving an image: The smart one. The responsible one. The steady one. Looking back, I don't blame that boy. He was learning. He didn't yet have the light to name the fear or step through it. And isn't that true for all of us?

You can only act on the light you've been given. When the light is dim, you default to safety. When fear clouds the lens, you mistake suppression for strength. That's what I did. And that night in the cafeteria wasn't the last time I stood still while the music played.

It's amazing—how these patterns begin. I wish I could say that moment was the last time fear dictated the terms.
But it wasn't.
It wasn't just about a dance.
It became a pattern—
one that didn't end in adolescence.

I got better at hiding it. I got good at replacing vulnerability with performance. Because that's what fear does when left unchecked. It doesn't just hold you back. It hands you a mask—and tells you to earn your worth while wearing it.

Here's the question I didn't ask until much later:

What if everything I was working so hard to prove…
was just a way to *avoid being seen*?

ACHIEVEMENT AS ARMOR

I wasn't ambitious. I was afraid. The fear disguised itself as drive. And most people praised the disguise.

That's the trap of fear-driven achievement. It looks like excellence. It sounds like ambition. It moves fast, speaks well, and earns applause. But underneath it all? Survival. I didn't chase success because I loved the climb. I chased it because I didn't want to be left behind.

Because deep down, I believed this:
If I fail, they'll see me.
And if they see me, they'll know I'm not enough.

That's the story I told myself. The only story I could tell—based on the limited light I had.

THE FEAR-DRIVEN ACHIEVER

So what is a fear-driven achiever? A fear-driven achiever isn't someone who's afraid to act. It's someone who acts constantly—so they don't have to feel afraid. We're not lazy. We're overloaded. We're not uncertain. We're overcompensating. We show up early. Stay late. Hit goals. Impress people. Not because we're fearless—but because we're afraid to stop.

We've quietly convinced ourselves that failure would expose who we really are. And here's the cruel irony: the reward for all that effort isn't joy. It's relief. Relief from the pressure. Relief from the fear. Relief that—for now—you didn't mess it up. But the pressure always returns. And every time, it builds higher than the last.

So you keep going. Not because you're inspired. But because you're afraid to stop. That D.L. Moody quote hits different when you're winning—but still feel hollow inside: "Our greatest fear should not be of failure, but of succeeding at something that doesn't really matter." Because success doesn't silence the inner critic. It feeds it.

It tells you the only way to matter is to keep performing. To keep proving. And that's how a life of proving begins. Because when you're doing something that "really matters," no one questions the pace, the pressure, or the cost.

But the cost compounds over time.

Let's look at how that story unfolds:

Childhood & Early School Years
- You try to be perfect, especially in areas where success feels safe.
- You avoid attention in unfamiliar settings.
- You overthink everything, hoping not to disappoint.

Junior High & High School
- You appear responsible, but inside you're scanning for risk.
- You avoid trying unless success feels guaranteed.
- You build an identity around not messing up.

College & Early Career
- You define yourself by grades, internships, or approval.
- You work twice as hard for half the peace.
- Your worth feels fragile, just one step from falling apart.

Midlife & Leadership
- You perform relentlessly. You can't turn it off.
- You avoid rest because stillness feels like weakness.
- Your identity becomes your resumé, the pressure never stops.

Fear-driven achievers often rise quickly. We look dependable, strategic, unshakable. Execution? Flawless. But the higher we climb, the more isolated we become. What started as effort becomes identity. And once you're seen as the one who always gets it done, very few people stop to ask if you're okay. Instead, you get more—more assignments. More expectations. More complexity.

The logic becomes suffocating: I'm here now. So I really can't afford to fail. So we don't scale back. We scale harder. We try to control the variables. We manage the narrative. The identity says, "This is who I am... because of what I do." We do everything we can to keep the image intact—even if we're unraveling inside. The identity we've built becomes too important to risk. Because if we stop, if we let go, we fear we'll lose not just the role—but the story that's held us together.

I wore my effort like armor. I was the dependable one. The high-achiever. The safe bet. The smart one. But the truth was quieter. I didn't feel like I could afford to rest. Because rest meant stopping. And stopping meant silence. And silence meant I'd hear the voice I didn't know how to shut out:

"You still haven't done enough."
"You still haven't done what really matters."

That's the voice fear uses when it wants to sound like wisdom. It doesn't have to scream. It just has to keep you moving. Like a whisper. Or a soft taunt. At first, the armor feels like strength. But over time, it gets heavy. You forget what it feels like to show up without the weight. You forget what it means to be seen without performance. You embrace the identity in one sense, but you lose yourself in another.

And maybe most painful of all—you forget that you were never made to hustle for love in the first place. So let me ask: What part of your identity is still performing for approval? What would it look like to lead without fear of exposure?

I didn't have language for it back then. I couldn't explain it. I just knew slowing down felt dangerous. Like if I stopped achieving, the version of me I had built might start to crack. So I kept the mask on. Smiled bigger. Hustled harder. Held more distance—so people wouldn't get close enough to see the truth. It wasn't about the goal anymore. It was about what achievement protected me from having to feel. So I wore the mask longer. And I ran harder.

Diagnostic Echo:
If I stopped proving myself... would there be anything real underneath?

That's what fear does best.
It hides in habits.
It blends into who you think you have to be.

You don't even notice it running your life—
until you're too tired to keep up.

THE INVISIBLE OPERATING SYSTEM

Fear doesn't always shout. Sometimes it just rewrites the rules—quietly, invisibly— until you start believing they've always been there. Don't mess it up. Keep it together. Be the responsible one. Stay ahead. Don't let them see you doubt. Do something that really matters. These aren't just thoughts. They're scripts. Unspoken codes, downloaded early, running constantly in the background like apps draining your battery. All day. Every day.

And we don't call it fear. We call it preparation. Work ethic. Excellence. Process. Discipline. Flawless execution. But sometimes what looks like discipline is just fear wearing a name tag that says *high standards*. Or in some cases—*perfectionism*. This is the invisible operating system. It doesn't ask for permission. It just runs. And the more successful you become, the more it adapts—constantly adjusting to keep control. So what does it look like in real life?

- A student who studies until 2 a.m. every night—not out of love for learning, but because one bad grade feels like the beginning of the end.
- A parent who never pauses to rest—not because they don't want to, but because they're terrified everything will fall apart without them.
- A manager who micromanages every detail—not because they don't trust their team, but because one mistake feels like a threat to their worth.
- A high-performer who keeps winning—but quietly wonders why every win feels emptier than the last.

These aren't failures of character. They're just signs that the system is running. Fear has embedded itself so deeply in your logic that you no longer question the pressure. You just obey it. Think about it:

- ☐ You hit a milestone… and feel pressure instead of joy.

- ☐ You get promoted… but now lie awake wondering how to prove you deserve it.

- ☐ You finish the project… but already feel behind on the next one.

You don't feel like you're growing. You feel like you're managing an image. That's what fear does best: It masquerades as motivation—while slowly rewiring your life around control, image, and output. And here's the hardest part:

> **Most people around you never know it's happening.**

Because on the outside, you're crushing it.

But on the inside?

Fear is holding the wheel. And you don't even realize you've handed over the keys.

THE VOICE YOU LEARN TO OBEY

You don't remember exactly when it started. That voice in your head—the one that doesn't yell, but always knows exactly what to say to keep you in line. Don't be dramatic. That's not what people like you do. Be easy to work with. Don't ask for too much. You should be grateful.

It doesn't sound like fear. It sounds like responsibility. Like realism. Like common sense. But if you listen closely, you might realize it's not truth at all. **It's your giant.** And it's been lying to you for years.

You didn't get that voice from nowhere. It started in small, forgettable moments:

- ☐ The disappointed look from a parent.
- ☐ The time you were laughed at for trying too hard.
- ☐ The A-minus that somehow felt like failure.
- ☐ The compliment that praised your performance—but ignored your personhood.

So you adapted. You learned what was acceptable. What was "too much." You started managing reactions instead of showing up honestly. Not because you were fake—but because you were afraid.

And over time, you internalized the rules:

1. **Keep it together.**
2. **Make it look easy.**
3. **Don't ask for help.**
4. **Make others proud.**

Eventually, you couldn't tell where your thoughts ended and their expectations began. And here's the trap: that voice doesn't just critique. It loops—like a bad roller coaster. You do something bold—then second-guess it. You rehearse how to fix it. You promise to be more "low key" next time. You speak up in a meeting—then lie awake replaying every word.

You get praised for being "calm and professional"—so you shrink again to stay consistent. The loop continues. The fear stays quiet. But it doesn't leave. That's the saddest part. We obey that voice because we think it's keeping us safe. But it's not keeping you safe. It's keeping you small. It's keeping you hidden—not just from risk, but from joy. From freedom. From being truly known.

And the longer you obey it, the harder it gets to see who you really are underneath. Because when you've listened long enough, even the giant starts to sound like you.

THE SIGNS YOU'VE BUILT A LIFE AROUND FEAR

You didn't mean to build your life around fear. But the voice was persistent. And convincing. Play it safe and you'll stay ahead. Achieve more and they'll never question you. Keep pushing—don't let them see you slip. You believed it. Not because you were weak. But because it sounded so true.

But now—if you pause long enough—you might start to see the signs. Not just in your thoughts, but in your schedule. Not just in your mood, but in your metrics. Not just in your head, but in your habits. You've been listening to the giant. And the giant has been lying to you. Because fear doesn't always build chaos. Sometimes, it builds success. Just not the kind that satisfies.

If you want to recognize it—look at the patterns:

Childhood and Adolescence
- You tried to be perfect—at whatever felt safe.
- You stuck to the things that earned approval.
- You avoided public failure like the plague.
- You made an inner vow: *That won't happen again.*
- You felt responsible all the time. And it wore you out.

College and Early Career
- You overprepared for everything—exams, interviews, even first dates.
- You built your identity on your résumé or relationships.
- You tied your worth to your performance.
- You worked twice as hard for half the self-worth.
- You feared being "found out" for not having it all together.

Midlife and Leadership
- You became someone others could count on—so you never let yourself fall apart.
- You smiled while silently managing anxiety, burnout, or imposter syndrome.
- You avoided rest. Not because you didn't want it—but because it made you feel unproductive.
- You got promoted for being the strong one—which only made it harder to show weakness.
- You didn't crave celebration. You craved relief.

Later Years
- You wonder if you missed something—some joy you never gave yourself permission to feel.
- You sometimes regret the risks you didn't take.
- You carry wisdom others admire—but pain they don't see.
- You fear that if you slow down, you'll become invisible.

Let me be clear: this isn't a checklist to shame you. It's a mirror to help you see. You didn't ask fear to write your script. But if you recognize yourself here— you have the power to revise it. Because once you realize the life you've built was shaped by a lie, you can begin building something more honest. More whole. More *you*.

And you're not alone. There are thousands—maybe millions—who've been shaped by fear-driven achievement, wearing it like armor. But that armor is not your identity. The hashtag fear gave you is not the name you have to live by.

THE COST OF SUCCESS WITHOUT SAFETY

You got the job. You won the award. You built the reputation. You became the one people counted on. You even got the title. But you never felt safe. There's a kind of success that feels like a tightrope. You're high up. The spotlight's on. Everyone's clapping, watching. But all you can think about is how far there is to fall. That's the cost of success without safety.

You work harder. Look stronger. Appear more in control. But inside, you're managing risk—not just the risk of failure—but the deeper risk: **being found out.** Because for the fear-driven achiever, the real terror isn't missing the mark. It's being seen.

So you become fluent in hiding exhaustion behind excellence. You master the art of looking fine. You say "I've got it," even when you don't. You push through the warning signs. You don't slow down—because slowing down feels dangerous. So you double down. Again. And again.

But over time, it adds up. You wake up tired. Your inner world is noisy—even in silence. You rehearse worst-case scenarios like it's your full-time job. You celebrate the win—but only for a moment. It's not joy. It's relief. Then you're onto the next.

Start asking yourself:
- Do I feel rested—or just less exhausted than usual?

- When I succeed, do I breathe deeply—or start planning what's next?

- Am I driven—or am I being chased?

These are the signs of quiet burnout. Of high-functioning anxiety wearing a high-achiever's smile. Of imposter syndrome whispering:

"Don't get too comfortable. This could all fall apart."

And if it does fall apart—what unravels isn't just your plan. It's your identity. That's what makes it so hard to name.

THE FEAR-DRIVEN ACHIEVER

You don't always have the language. But you feel it. That low-level dread. That tension under the surface. That edge you live on. And underneath it all is a cycle you've never quite escaped:

- **Intention** leads to disruption.
  You set a bold goal. You raise the stakes. You step out.
- **Disruption** stirs emotion.
  Anticipation. Insecurity. Excitement. Fear.

But for the fear-driven achiever, emotion feels unsafe. It's a liability to manage, not a companion to guide.

- **Emotion** triggers a loss of clarity.
  You forget your "why." You reach for control. You tighten your grip.
- **Control** becomes the coping mechanism. You double down on performance, image, and outcomes.

And so the cycle begins again:
More intention.
More disruption.
More emotion.
Less clarity.

You keep moving forward—but the cost is compounding. So you quietly start to ask: *Why doesn't it feel like I belong here? Why do I feel behind even when I'm ahead? Why can't I stop proving—even to myself?*

This is the ache behind the accolades. You made it. But you never got to rest. You won. But you never felt peace. Because when fear is your fuel, success becomes a performance—not a place you get to live.

But there's another way. And it begins with one question: **What would it take to feel safe—not just successful?**

THE QUESTION BEHIND THE HUSTLE

Do you even know who you are without the fear? You've spent your life chasing the next thing. The next win. The next rung. The next version of yourself that might finally feel like enough. But if you stopped—even for a moment—what would be left?

There's a silence that terrifies the fear-driven achiever. It's not the silence of failure. It's the silence of no audience. No one to impress. No milestone to reach. No scoreboard to check. Just stillness.

And the question you've been outrunning for years:

If I'm not proving myself... who am I?

THE FEAR-DRIVEN ACHIEVER

See, when the applause fades and the pressure lifts, there's no identity left to manage. No performance to perfect. And in that absence, a deeper echo rings out. Not in noise—but in quiet. If I stopped achieving, if I stopped building, if I stopped striving…would there be anything real underneath? That's the question behind the hustle. And it's not just for high performers.

> It's for parents.
> For students.
> For pastors and teachers and team leaders.
> For retirees.

For anyone who's ever tied their value to being responsible, impressive, reliable, or in control. Because fear doesn't always stop you. Sometimes, it drives you forward—fast and furious—so you never have to pause long enough to ask if your worth is conditional.

Many of us live like we're only as valuable as our last success. Our last win. Our last contribution. So we keep proving. Because we don't want to find out what happens if we don't. But eventually, something cracks. The job changes. The relationship shifts. The body gives out. The role you built your identity around disappears. And what's underneath… isn't failure. It's emptiness. That's when many achievers panic.

But that's also where healing begins. Because what feels like collapse is often the invitation to rebuild. Not a better version of you. A truer one. This is the moment. The place where striving starts to break down. And you begin to ask: Who am I without the mask? Who was I before the hustle? You were never meant to prove your worth. You were meant to live from it. But to do that, you'll have to go back and name the fear.

Not just the fear of failure. But the deeper one—the fear that without your hustle, you might disappear. Somewhere along the way, you started believing that what you do *is* who you are. You built a life chasing success because asking what really matters felt too vulnerable. But as D.L. Moody once said:

"Our greatest fear should not be of failure, but of succeeding at something that doesn't really matter."

And maybe—just maybe—for the first time, you're seeing the sky crack open. Not all the way. Not clear and calm. But just enough to let in a sliver of light. Because that's what truth does. It breaks through.

What would it take to live without the lie? What would it look like to be free—not just impressive? What would it mean to walk not just in success—but in purpose? The next chapter won't promise ease. But it does promise clarity. And clarity is worth the cost.

WHERE WE GO FROM HERE

If you've made it this far, you've likely felt something start to unravel. That's good. Not in a way that destroys—but in a way that reveals. Because maybe the story you've been living isn't the whole truth. And perhaps—you're starting to wonder: What if I've been chasing something that never had the power to name me?

This book isn't about becoming fearless. It's about becoming honest. It's about learning to name the fear—not just to remove it, but to discover what's been hiding underneath. Because when you peel back fear-driven achievement, you don't find laziness. Or weakness. Or failure.

You find a younger version of you—doing the best they could with the light they had. You don't need to shame them. You don't need to bury them. You need to listen to them. Because that voice? It isn't just a liability. It's a landmark.

It marks the moment you stopped trusting yourself. The moment you started outsourcing your identity. The moment fear whispered: *"Play it safe and you'll stay accepted."* But you're not that version anymore. You've seen too much. You've named too much. You've lost too much. And you've gained something fear can't steal:

Clarity.

Clarity about who you are.

Clarity about what matters.

Clarity that success without purpose is just performance in disguise. And purpose—real purpose—isn't earned by hustle. It's received through identity. So no, this isn't where your story ends. This is where the real story begins.

From here forward, we'll walk through the names you've been given—and the name fear never wanted you to discover. Because your giants have been lying to you.

But now?

You know how to listen for the truth.

DOUBLING DOWN IN UNIFORM

After college, I stepped out into a world still reeling from the 2008 Great Financial Crisis. Armed with a business degree and a gnawing sense of "not enough," I entered the workforce during a time when jobs were scarce and certainty felt abstract. I wanted to serve. I wanted to lead. I wanted to matter. But underneath all that desire, I mostly didn't want to fail.

My brothers had joined the Army National Guard, and something about their path lit a spark in me. I discovered a role called Civil Affairs Specialist. It sounded bold. Strategic. Noble. Different – the kind of role that bridged humanitarian work and military service. It was a position in the U.S. Army Reserve—not quite the same as my brothers. And that mattered to me.

It felt like a calling. But looking back, I realize something else was driving me. It wasn't just purpose. It was fear—wearing a new uniform. At the time, I would've told you I was stepping into destiny. But in reality, I was still obeying the old script:

"You cannot fail. You must not fall behind."

So I made a move that looked courageous—but was really about control. About stability. About approval. About finding a path that felt respectable and reliable. And in many ways, it worked. It earned admiration. It gave me structure. It made people take notice. But it also gave fear a new costume. And I wore it well.

I didn't know it then, but I was still living out the first half of the evangelist D.L. Moody's warning: "Our greatest fear should not be of failure…" That was my operating system. Fear was the fuel. It would take years—and eventually, a limp—to understand the second half of the quote: "…but of succeeding at something that doesn't really matter." It's not that the military didn't matter. It certainly does. It was that **I didn't know who I was apart from what I could prove.** I had confused mission with identity. Calling with image.

On paper, I was succeeding. But behind the scenes, I was unraveling. I was doing the job. But I was breaking in ways I didn't yet understand. That limp didn't just come from training. It came from trying to prove who I was—until my body forced me to stop.

Most people don't carry visible scars from the battlefield. But almost all of us carry bruises from the war within – the kind no medal can recognize. *You're not weak for being afraid. But you are free to stop obeying fear.* So let me ask: Where in your life have you confused achievement with identity? What decision looked like courage—but was actually about control?

Chapter 2

THE INJURY THAT CHANGED EVERYTHING

THE FIRST SIGNS: WHEN YOUR BODY KNOWS BEFORE YOU DO

Sometimes, fear doesn't announce itself with a breakdown in your emotions. Sometimes, it breaks your body first.

Army Basic Training was disorienting—intense, fast-paced, everything still new. Then, without warning, our company got pulled into a physical confidence course earlier than scheduled. One of those team-building gauntlets designed to test your limits and bond you fast.

The final obstacle was a towering wooden structure meant to test physical ability, team problem solving, and resilience—no ladders, no ropes, just a series of staggered platforms spaced seven or eight feet apart, rising 15 to 25 feet into the air. You weren't climbing it alone. That was the point.

At 6'2", I was one of the bigger guys, so I stayed behind to help lift soldier after soldier to the first level. When it was my turn, we had a plan: I'd reach up, they'd grab my arms, I'd swing my legs up, they'd catch them and pull.

Brilliant. Until it wasn't.

They missed my legs.

I swung forward like a wrecking ball—my hip crashing into the wooden beam with full force. I was left dangling. Blinking. Dazed. Something deep inside felt wrong. Off. I didn't know what had happened, but I knew something had shifted. I ignored it.

From that moment on, I started limping—barely at first, then noticeably. The pain followed behind the limp like a shadow that kept gaining weight. But I didn't stop. I didn't slow down. I didn't say a word. I pressed harder. Because in my mind, the limp meant losing. And I couldn't afford to fail.

My identity was wrapped tightly around being a Civil Affairs soldier, a US Army-based humanitarian who can make a real difference. This was the dream. The calling. And if I stopped—even for a moment—I risked losing it all. That wasn't an option. I didn't realize it yet, but that injury wasn't just physical. It was a marker. The moment grit quietly fractured into grief. And I refused to listen.

THE COLLAPSE OF CAPACITY

The signs came subtly at first:

- ✓ Sleepless nights.
- ✓ Numb tingling in my leg that never quite went away.
- ✓ Sudden spasms jerking me awake.
- ✓ A deep ache that stretching, rest, and resolve couldn't touch.

But the story I told myself was louder:

> **Push through it.**
> **It'll pass.**
> **You're fine.**

I told myself that every day—sometimes every hour. That the pain was temporary. That others had it worse. That rest was weakness. That to succeed, I had to keep going.

The limp was visible now, impossible to hide. But the real limp was beneath the surface—buried in the belief that I had to finish strong or not at all. There's not much space for reflection in basic training. So I didn't reflect.

> I wrapped myself tighter in discipline.
> In grit.
> In shame.
> I masked the pain.
> I altered my stride.

I told myself I'd recover after graduation.

Whenever someone asked if I was okay, my answer was always the same: "Yes." But my body had other plans. The pain got worse. Sharper. Constant.

I tried everything short of stopping—ice packs after training, Tylenol to dull the edges. At first, it worked. Then it didn't. Eventually, I hit the maximum dosage. Even then, the pain kept rising.

Somewhere along the way, I normalized it.

Pain became my scoreboard.

If I could still feel it, I thought, that meant I hadn't pushed too far. If the pain faded, I assumed I'd crossed into dangerous territory—where real damage lived. So I used the pain as my proof: proof I was still in control. Proof I hadn't broken anything too badly.

But the limp wasn't manageable anymore.
It was unmissable.
Still—I refused to stop.
Refused to ask for help.

Because stopping meant admitting something was broken. And in the fear-driven world I was living in, broken meant failure.

THE QUIET PANIC – HOW ACHIEVERS REACT TO PHYSICAL LIMITATION

You don't realize how loud the silence is until your body stops cooperating. I made it. Somehow, I pushed through basic training, through advanced training, through every drill and march and evaluation—limping, hurting, but never stopping. I crossed the finish line. And I wore the title with pride: **U.S. Army Reserve Civil Affairs Specialist.**

I hoped that once I got home, things would ease up. I'd only be drilling once a month. Surely the pain would fade now. Surely. But life moved fast. I returned to my civilian job—unloading trucks at a grocery store, moving pallets of dairy and frozen goods. Hundreds of pounds stacked six feet high, shoved down narrow aisles on slick floors. Shift after shift, I told myself this wasn't like basic. I wasn't running. I wasn't in full combat gear. This was easier. Right?

I thought my intention—to work hard, to recover, to keep going—would make the difference. But intention doesn't cancel reality. It only delays the crash. For a while, the pain seemed to ease. The limp softened. False hope.

By noon each day, I was maxed out on Tylenol and Aleve again. Still limping. Still aching. Still pretending I was getting better. And now—I wasn't invisible anymore. My team noticed. My managers. Customers. My family. No one said anything. But I could feel it.

I felt slower. Exposed. Like I was falling behind in the very life I had fought to return to. Tasks took longer. Stress climbed higher. Performance dropped—and so did my pride. My intention had become disruption. And that disruption stirred something I kept trying to push deeper and deeper down. A rising fear I couldn't name yet, but that was starting to cloud my vision and choke my clarity. That's when the quiet panic crept in.

Not just the fear that I was in pain—but the fear that I was changing. I wasn't just hurting. I was becoming someone I didn't recognize. Fragile. Falling behind. Maybe even… failing.
What if I couldn't bounce back?
What if I couldn't fulfill my commitment?
What if everything I'd sacrificed, everything I'd endured—wasn't enough?

Then came the moment I could no longer deny:
I needed surgery.
I needed help.
I couldn't fix this myself.

This wasn't about pushing through anymore. This wasn't about proving anything. This was surrender—not to defeat, but to truth. And truth whispered something I had spent months avoiding:

You can't outrun this.

THE ANATOMY OF A BREAKING POINT: WHEN PRETENDING COSTS TOO MUCH

You can lie to your mind longer than you can lie to your body. There wasn't some dramatic fall. No ambulance. No cinematic collapse in the middle of a grocery store aisle. But there *was* a moment. And it was final.

I don't remember the exact day—only that it started like every other. I was pushing pallets. Gripping the handle a little tighter. Adjusting to the limp I'd grown used to. Pretending I wasn't holding my breath with every step. I acted out the same rehearsed cycle. By noon, max dose of pain relievers, but maximum pain. Still limping. Still aching. Still pretending. But that day, something shifted.

For just a second, I stopped moving—stood still. And in that stillness, clarity finally broke through.

**This isn't getting better.
It's getting worse.**

It wasn't a fearful thought. It was a truthful one. That was the moment effort stopped being brave and started being expensive. That was the moment pretending to be strong started costing more than the courage it would take to ask for help. And that was the day I said it out loud:

"I need surgery. I can't keep doing this."

It wasn't the end of my ambition. It was the end of the illusion. The lie that I could hustle my way out of injury. That I could outthink pain. Outperform limitation. Out-grit the physical reality of my body breaking down. I had crossed a line—not just physically, but emotionally. For the first time in months, I didn't try to step back. I didn't shift the narrative. I didn't reframe the pain. I just told the truth.

What stories have you told yourself about how life *should* work—like if you work hard, stay strong, and do the right things, everything will turn out okay?

When those formulas stop delivering, can you tell the truth… or do you still try to make the equation fit?

THE ILLUSION OF THE FORMULA: WHEN A+B DOESN'T EQUAL SUCCESS

They told us if we did A, B, and C… we'd get X, Y, and Z.
Work hard → succeed.
Do the right thing → everything works out.
Push through the pain → earn the reward.

But no one tells you what to do when the formula stops working. From an early age, I believed in outcomes. Effort equaled progress. Good choices led to good results. That belief gave me fuel. It gave the fear-driven hustle a purpose. It made pain feel productive. It made me feel like it was all worth it.

THE INJURY THAT CHANGED EVERYTHING

Even after the injury. Even when surgery became inevitable. Even when the truth became too loud to ignore. I still believed the formula would hold. I thought if I just kept pushing—kept showing up, kept gritting it out—then eventually it would pay off. The pain would turn into progress. The sacrifice would become strength. The hard road would still get me to the life I'd imagined. But that's not how it happened.

I didn't bounce back. I didn't feel victorious. And worse—I didn't feel like myself anymore. Even the *version* of myself I had carefully crafted—the image, the drive, the purpose-tied-to-performance—it didn't fit anymore. That's the hidden cost of believing in linear success: When the formula fails, you don't just lose your strength. You lose your story.

I had to face a harder truth: I wasn't broken because I failed the formula. I was broken because I believed the formula guaranteed success in the first place. And when that belief collapsed, I didn't just feel tired. I felt betrayed.

Have you ever followed the "right steps" and still ended up broken, lost, or disappointed?

What if the failure wasn't in *you*—but in the formula you were taught to trust?

THE TURNING TABLE: AN UNEXPECTED DOOR INTO A NEW STORY

Sometimes, the next chapter doesn't start with inspiration. It starts with an intake form. In a quiet hallway that smells like antiseptic. Surgery forced me to stop. But healing? Healing forced me to *slow down*—in a way I never had before.

Eight weeks on crutches. Non-weight-bearing. The first four weeks spent wearing a hip brace to keep the joint from dislocating. Even basic tasks—like getting to the bathroom in the middle of the night—required help. For someone used to proving, pushing, and performing…that kind of dependency didn't just feel uncomfortable. It felt like failure.

No more hiding. No more outrunning. Just stillness. Surrender. And unexpectedly… space. I did my physical therapy at a small community hospital. It wasn't glamorous. It wasn't tied to any title. It was awkward. Repetitive. Quiet. And yet… something began to shift.

One day, the front desk receptionist looked up and smiled: "You always show up on time. You give it your all. You should come work here." I laughed. Internally, I dismissed it completely.

I didn't see myself as someone who worked at a hospital.

THE INJURY THAT CHANGED EVERYTHING

I was still clinging to the dream—if I healed fast enough, worked hard enough, maybe I could still get back to the Army. Back to Civil Affairs. Back to the purpose I thought I'd lost. I didn't realize it yet, but I was still stuck in the fear-driven achiever mindset. Still trying to *earn* my way back to the original story. But halfway through physical therapy, reality caught up.

The grocery store? It wasn't an option anymore. My body wouldn't make it through a single shift. The pain wouldn't allow it. I started searching frantically for something—*anything*—I could physically handle. Something that didn't require combat boots or 10-hour shifts on concrete floors. And slowly, it began to dawn on me: If I couldn't make it through a civilian shift…How could I possibly return to the Army?

Then, by what I now know was divine providence, I came across a job posting—in that same hospital. The supply chain department. A behind-the-scenes role. Stocking and distributing. Order and logistics. It wasn't glamorous. It wasn't what I had trained for. It wasn't even what I thought I wanted. But it was open. And I was ready.

My identity had crumbled—but in the rubble, I could see the outline of something new. It was an unexpected door. One I didn't plan for. One I hadn't earned. One I almost missed. It wasn't fast. It wasn't linear. It didn't look anything like the future I imagined when I first put on the uniform.

But it was real. And it was *mine*. I was still limping. Still healing. Still uncertain. But I wasn't aimless anymore. Something deeper had begun to take root—not a five-year plan, not a title, but a sense that maybe life was still moving forward. Just not in the way I scripted it. And maybe… maybe purpose wasn't something I had to chase.

Maybe it was something I was meant to *live*. Not in future promotions. Not in some overseas deployment. But right here. In how I showed up. In what I built. In who I impacted. Maybe purpose wasn't about the spotlight. Maybe it looked more like quiet consistency. Less hustle. More helping.

I hadn't lost my purpose. I had just been running too fast to see where it was trying to take me. I wasn't chasing anymore. I was planting. Building. Stewarding what was right in front of me. And in that slower rhythm… something unexpected happened. I didn't feel off track anymore. I felt… *aligned*. Maybe for the first time.

Have you ever found yourself standing in a place you didn't plan to be—wounded, uncertain, off-script—but strangely… more grounded?

What if purpose isn't about chasing the perfect story, but noticing the door that's quietly opened right in front of you?

WHEN CALLING COLLAPSES, PURPOSE CLARIFIES

You didn't fail when the plan fell apart. You just discovered it wasn't the whole story.

For years, I thought my purpose was public service. Civil Affairs. Helping people. Wearing the uniform. It gave me direction. It gave me status. And more than that—it gave me meaning. I was doing something that mattered. But after the injury… after the limp… after the surgery… after being redirected into a hospital supply chain job I never asked for—I had to face something hard: what I thought was **purpose** was really just **calling**. And calling had changed.

Calling is an *assignment*. It's seasonal. Situational. Sometimes specific. But purpose? Purpose is deeper. Purpose is why you're here—not where you're placed. When my assignment collapsed, the fear-driven part of me panicked: What now? Was it all wasted? Do I still matter if I'm not doing what I was trained for?

But slowly, as I kept showing up—brace off. Crutches down. Walking slower, but straighter—I began to see something sacred forming beneath the rubble. I was still bringing order to chaos. Still supporting a mission bigger than me. Still serving real people with real needs. The uniform changed. But the impact? It stayed.

And that's when the truth finally broke through:

Purpose is planted.
Calling is assigned.
Purpose is who you are.
Calling is what you do.

When calling collapses, purpose doesn't die. It just gets revealed. You didn't fail when the plan fell apart. You just found out it wasn't the whole story.

THE WRESTLE: ENTERING JACOB'S STORY

There comes a point when what you *do* can no longer carry who you *are*.

By the time I stepped into the hospital supply chain job, I had shed more than just a limp. I had shed a version of myself I spent years building—the image. The drive. The assignment. The uniform. The future I thought I had secured. But the internal wrestle hadn't ended. If anything, it was just beginning.

Shortly after starting my new job, the Army initiated a formal medical review. Over the next year, I was pulled back into the process—scans. Evaluations. Physical therapy. Paperwork. More waiting. Eventually, the decision came down:

No longer fit to serve. Honorably discharged. Done.

DISABLED. Rated at 60% capable.

I stared at that number longer than I care to admit.

60%

Not a medical diagnosis—but a quiet verdict: you're no longer whole. You're 60% of a man. That label haunted me. I had given everything I had not to fail. And yet, somehow, the final score still said:

Less.

I kept showing up at work. I learned new systems. Moved supplies. Supported clinicians. Helped patients. But underneath the steady rhythm of serving others, I was silently asking questions I didn't know how to answer:

Who am I now?

What do I have to offer if I'm not at full capacity?

What's my value if I'm not mission ready?

And that— not the injury, not the surgery, not even the discharge—**that** was the real breaking point. Because the deepest pain wasn't physical. It was identity-level.

I thought I was rebuilding.
But I was about to begin **wrestling**—not with pain.
With **purpose**.
With **identity**.
With **God**.

Genesis 32 tells of a man named Jacob, a biblical patriarch, whose identity was forever changed at the turning point where purpose, identity, and God collided. Jacob's story begins right where mine left off—a lone figure standing at the edge of everything he built, face to face with the one thing he couldn't outmaneuver:

The truth about who he really was.

And that's when the wrestle began…

Chapter 3

JACOB'S WRESTLE: FIGHTING FOR IDENTITY

STUCK BETWEEN WHAT BROKE YOU AND WHAT MIGHT KILL YOU

The night before everything changes…

Jacob, the biblical patriarch, son of Isaac, grandson of Abraham, wasn't just heading toward reunion. He was walking into reckoning. Ahead of him stood Esau, his older twin brother — the brother he had deceived, the one whose last words to Jacob had been a vow of revenge.

Behind Jacob was Laban, his manipulative father-in-law, who twisted every agreement, changed his wages ten times, and nearly convinced him to stay just one more year… one more scheme… one more cycle in a toxic environment. Jacob wasn't chasing something hopeful.

YOUR GIANTS ARE LYING TO YOU

He was running from what had broken him… and bracing for what might destroy him. He wasn't free. He was cornered. And that night, as he reached the edge of the Jabbok River, described in Genesis 32:22-32, both ghosts caught up with him.

For the first time in a long time, there were no more strategies to play, no more deals to cut, no one left to blame. Just darkness. Just silence. Just Jacob. Alone.

What do you do when going back means a slow death—but going forward might kill you faster?

This wasn't peaceful solitude. This was panic disguised as stillness. Jacob had already sent his wives, his children, his livestock — everything he owned and loved — across the river. His legacy. His future. His entire life. But he stayed behind. And in that pause, in the still gap between movement and meaning, he didn't just face a decision. He faced himself.

This moment wasn't about geography. It was about identity. It wasn't about Esau or Laban. It was about Jacob. Because even though he was moving forward, he wasn't free. Not yet. Not really. He still carried the echo of his old names —Deceiver. Manipulator. Striver. Heel-grabber (the literal meaning of Jacob's name). Yes, he had survived — but only by becoming someone he wasn't proud of. Someone who outworked pain, out planned rejection, outran shame.

Or so he thought.

That night at the river, the hustle ran out. It's like walking away from a job that drained you — where you gave years of your life and identity — only to step into the unknown with no guarantees you'll survive. Jacob's story isn't just ancient. It's achingly modern, the patterns still repeat in leadership, relationships, and identity today.

It's the high achiever burned by a narcissistic boss, now second-guessing every move, still susceptible to every manipulative hook because failure isn't an option. It's the survivor of a toxic relationship stepping into something new — cautious, afraid, still carrying the weight of the old story. It's the leader trying to inspire others while secretly wrestling with burnout, hiding behind a thick armor no one sees through. It's the 2 a.m. ceiling stare —

"Who am I if I'm not hustling?"

"What if I let go… and it all falls apart?"

"What if what I fear most isn't out there — but in here?"

Jacob wasn't just afraid of Esau. He was afraid of who he might be without the armor. Without the fight. Without the mask. Without the plan. You can be exhausted by your past and still terrified of your future.

That's where transformation begins.

This was the night before the name change. Before the limp. Before the shift that would ripple through history — all the way to you. And this is the night every fear-driven achiever eventually faces. When what used to work… stops. When the ghosts behind still whisper. And the giants ahead still glare. But in the middle — in the stillness—something holy happens.

You stop moving. You stop fixing. You stop pretending. And you stand in the terrifying, sacred tension. Who will I be if I don't go back? Who am I becoming if I go forward?

You don't need to know Jacob's story to know what it feels like to be stuck between a ghost and a giant. You've felt it. In your chest. In your gut. In the quiet hours when the world sleeps and only your voice remains. You won't find this kind of moment in your Instagram story highlights. You won't see it on TikTok. But it's real. And it's where the story begins to shift — If you choose to face it…instead of repeating the cycle. This is the beginning of everything.

THE WOUND IN THE DARK WHAT BREAKS YOU MIGHT BE WHAT SAVES YOU

Jacob came into the night ready to fight — not because he wanted to, but because that's all he knew. Survival had become second nature. Doubling down had become his default. He had built his whole life on grabbing what didn't come easy: Birthrights. Blessings. Wages. Women. Wealth.

He knew how to scheme. He knew how to run. He knew how to win. But that night, he met someone he couldn't outmaneuver. Scripture tells us a man wrestled with Jacob until daybreak. No name. No warning. Just sudden, relentless impact. This wasn't a sparring match. This was a soul struggle. Jacob wasn't strategizing anymore. He was surviving. And for once, winning had nothing to do with cleverness. It had everything to do with holding on.

Fear-driven achievers are built for this moment. We know how to fight. We know how to push through pain. We know how to pretend we're fine while breaking inside. We are determined to give whatever it takes to get the outcome we desire.

But this wasn't a negotiation. It wasn't a hustle. It wasn't even a test. It was transformation. And Jacob's wiring wouldn't let him surrender. So something had to give. And it did. A blow to the hip. Dislocation. Collapse. Not because Jacob was weak — but because he wouldn't let go. Sometimes God breaks what you won't surrender. The wound wasn't punishment. It was mercy.

Because without it, Jacob would have kept wrestling — for control, for validation, for the win. But when his hip gave out, the hustle did too.

That dislocation—the moment when strength snapped—wasn't the end. It was the beginning of the shift.

Jacob didn't lose. He survived. And survival required surrender. Fear-driven achievers will double down until something breaks. That's not weakness. That's grace. Jacob's limp wasn't failure. It was the only thing that could stop his striving. And many of us live by the same unspoken rules:

> *"If I let go, I'll lose everything."*
> *"If I slow down, I'll fall behind."*
> *"If I show weakness, they won't take me seriously…not my staff. Not my friends. Not my family."*

So we keep pushing—until something gives. The body breaks. The marriage cracks. The anxiety spikes. The heart flutters. The exhaustion floors us. And in that moment, it doesn't feel like mercy. It feels like collapse. And to the fear-driven achiever, collapse is unacceptable.

But what if collapse isn't failure? What if it's the signal that something deeper is trying to get your attention? Here's what most high achievers miss: the wound you didn't choose might be the very thing that saves you—not from pain, but from pretending. It's like working nonstop until your body finally says, "No more."

Until the diagnosis. Until the breakdown. Until the betrayal.

And you realize: I can't go back to how I used to live. Something's clearer now. And you stand at a threshold — move forward in truth, or return to the cycle that broke you. At the start of the wrestling, Jacob still thought he could win his way into blessing. But now? His hip is shattered. His strength is gone. The sun is rising. And he's clinging not from power—but from desperation.

This is the turning point. This is where blessing doesn't come through achievement. It comes through breaking. The limp isn't loss. It's the mark of a different kind of strength. From that moment forward, Jacob would never walk the same again. But he wouldn't walk in fear. He wouldn't walk under the pressure to prove. He wouldn't walk with his old name still clinging to him like a cheap name tag.

> He would walk wounded… but free.
> For the first time in his life,
> He didn't have to pretend he was whole.

So let me ask:
When did your title become armor?

And what finally forced you to lay it down?

THE NEW NAME WHEN SURRENDER BECOMES YOUR IDENTITY

Jacob's name literally meant "heel-grabber." It was stamped on him from birth—a name that told a story: You'll always have to chase. You'll always have to fight. You'll always be second—unless you find a way to cheat your way forward. It was a name built on striving. And for a long time, it worked.

He schemed his way into his brother's blessing. He outmaneuvered Laban for his wealth. He hustled until he had something to show for all the pain. But after the breaking… After the limp… After the long night of wrestling… Jacob wasn't the same. Something *holy* happened at daybreak.

"Your name shall no longer be called Jacob, but Israel —
For you have struggled with God and with men, and have prevailed."

>God didn't give Jacob a title. He gave him a name.
>Not a name he earned.
>Not a name he stole.
>Not a name he performed for.
>Not a name he had to hustle to achieve.

A name that said: You don't have to be who you were anymore. And it called him toward a future identity—one not shaped by fear or performance.

Sometimes your breakthrough isn't a new opportunity. It's a new name—for who you've become after the breaking. This wasn't branding. It was becoming. We live in a world obsessed with self-definition—personality tests. Job titles. Instagram bios. Follower counts. Likes. Public wins. We treat identity like a product. Like the next viral hashtag. The next TikTok trend. But Jacob's story says otherwise.

Your real name—the one worth living from — might not come until after everything breaks. You don't need to know the details of Jacob's story to know what it feels like to be renamed by pain. To realize the name you've been living under…no longer fits who you're becoming. To feel like the life you've built doesn't align with the soul that survived the breaking.

Before you go viral, get real.
Before you build a platform, find your foundation.

Jacob became Israel — not because he won — but because he *stayed in it*. He didn't run. He didn't tap out. He didn't let go. He limped through the night and held on. And that's what God renamed.

Not perfection.
Not polish.
Not fear-driven achievement.
Perseverance through pain.

For the fear-driven achiever, this is the shift. You've been trying to earn a name through performance — to silence the old names: Failure. Not enough. Imposter. You've tried to drown them out by collecting trophies.

Nods.
Likes.
Wins.

But the blessing didn't come through winning.
It came through *witness*.
Through wrestling.
Through not walking away.

You don't lead well by hiding your limp. You lead well when your scars stop being your secret — and start becoming your story. Before you lead others with confidence, you must walk with the limp that tells the truth.

Jacob's new name wasn't a finish line. It was an invitation. An invitation to live as someone who no longer needed to grab, deceive, or prove. But it was still Jacob's choice to embrace it. He walked away from the river renamed — but not yet restored. That would take time. But from that moment on, he would move differently. Not just because of the limp — but because of what the limp *meant*. Everywhere he walked, it echoed that moment. A reminder of who he was becoming.

So let me ask:
What name have you been trying to earn?
And what if the name that matters most—
the one that frees you—can't be earned at all?

If you're exhausted from trying to be someone online, maybe it's time to ask who are you… when no one's watching?

THE SCAR THAT SPEAKS THE MARK YOU DIDN'T ASK FOR AND CAN'T IGNORE

Jacob limped away from the encounter as the sun rose.
Scarred.
Renamed.
Forever changed.

That limp wasn't weakness. It was a marker. A physical echo of the moment he stopped hiding. Stopped running. And wrestled his way into truth. No crown. No fanfare. No applause. No trending view count. Just a wound he couldn't ignore — a wound that wouldn't let him forget: You are not the same.

For many of us — myself included — scars aren't symbolic. They're real. Mine run across my hip, the legacy of two surgeries that reshaped my life. I remember the first time I saw it — raw, swollen, angry. It didn't feel redemptive. It felt like defeat. I didn't want a scar. I wanted strength. But there it was — a physical reminder of what I'd been through.

Here's the truth: Healing doesn't ask for your permission. And scars don't wait until you're ready. Over time, the pain faded. But the scar stayed. It still does. And now? I don't just see a wound. I see a *witness*. A witness to survival. To surrender. To a transformation I never wanted… but somehow needed. And I'm grateful.

Your scars don't tell the story of your defeat. They tell the story of your fight. Your shift. Your survival. The hope of your transformation. We all carry scars. Some are visible. Some are buried. A breakup that left you questioning your worth. A career collapse that shattered your confidence. A trauma that never made the news but reshaped your soul. A betrayal that changed how you walk through the world.

Not all wounds bleed.

Some hide under perfectly functioning armor. But if you listen closely — even the invisible ones speak. Scars are like superhero origin stories. They mark the chapter where pain became personal — and the person became powerful. If they choose to. Think of Tony Stark's arc reactor — the damage that became destiny because he chose to embrace it. Or professional athletes with knees full of hardware and hearts full of fire because they refused to quit. Or leaders who carry wounds in body and spirit — and forged a legacy from them.

Jacob's limp wasn't just a mark of damage. It was the beginning of his destiny. And the foundation of his legacy. This wasn't just a religious moment. It was a human one. A man finally came face-to-face with the truth — of who he was. And who he wasn't. He couldn't cheat his way out. He couldn't perform his way through. He couldn't scheme his way into blessing. All he could do was wrestle – break – receive - and choose to walk in the new.

And leaders — hear this: your scars don't weaken your authority. They *authenticate* it. They don't disqualify your leadership. They prove you've lived through what others are still trying to name. That's your opportunity — to guide. To build. To lead from the middle of the story, not the illusion of a finish line.

You don't have to believe in God to recognize this: sometimes life doesn't ask for your permission — and still leaves a scar. You look in the mirror and hardly recognize the version of you that *survived*. But maybe that scar? It's not your shame. It's your signal.

> So let me ask: What scar do you carry that once felt like the end…but now whispers of a beginning?

Because transformation often leaves a mark. We don't limp because we're broken. We limp because we became.

NAMING THE NEW YOU: YOU DIDN'T LOSE YOURSELF – YOU SURVIVED TO BECOME SOMEONE NEW

Jacob's fight didn't end in triumph. It ended in a wound… and a name. The man who had deceived his way forward, who had spent decades striving, manipulating, and proving, was now limping into a new dawn.

Not victorious, but *seen*. Not polished, but *renamed*. Not defeated, but *hopeful*. And none of it came from reputation. Not from a resume, not from virality, not from a platform moment. It came from a private struggle no one else witnessed. From a God who saw him — dust-covered, breath ragged, clinging to hope with the last bit of strength he had left.

> *"Your name shall no longer be called Jacob, but Israel — for you have struggled with God and with men and have prevailed."*

We think names are given at birth —
by parents,
by culture,
by accident.

But sometimes your real name — the one that reflects who you're becoming — comes after the breaking. After the collapse. After the armor falls away and something truer begins to rise.

JACOB'S WRESTLE: FIGHTING FOR IDENTITY

Before you build a life around who you *think* you should be, wrestle for the name of who you actually *are*. In today's culture, we're told: create a brand before you find your voice. Chase a platform before you find your foundation. Get likes before you know what you truly like. Be seen before you even know how to see yourself. We're taught to perform. To achieve. Even if it's driven by fear.

But Jacob didn't get rebranded. He got *renamed*. And not for appearances — for *substance*. For the fear-driven achiever, this is where the illusion starts to crack open. You've been hustling for validation. Wearing name tags like "Not Enough." "Try Harder." "Proven." But maybe the thing that sidelined you — the diagnosis, the collapse, the shift you didn't ask for — is finally giving you permission… to stop performing. To stop doubling down. To stop chasing flawless execution.

This is where the mask breaks. Where the striving quiets. Where something inside you whispers:

> *You are no longer who you were.*
> *You don't have to hustle to matter.*
> *You're not defined by what broke you.*
> *You're named by what you **survived**.*

The name you need doesn't come through credentials or charisma. It comes in the dark, when everything else has fallen away, and grace meets you there with a whisper:
> *Live from who I've called you now to be.*

It won't come fully formed. It's not a finished brand.
It's a living name you grow into.
A limp you choose to carry.
A story you choose to walk out.
So choose it. **Break the cycle.**

Because here's the truth: titles can feel like armor — impressive on the outside, but heavy and hollow when fear is driving the inside. Jacob didn't become Israel because he got promoted. He became Israel because he stopped pretending. Leadership rooted in image will always collapse under pressure. But leadership born from identity—from inner purpose—endures.

So let me ask: What would you change if you led from who you are instead of who they expect you to be?

For me, the scar isn't metaphorical. It's literal. After injury and surgery, I was left with a limp I couldn't hide. My performance was limited. My energy had to be rationed. And slowly… something deeper began to rise. Not in spite of the pain, but *because* of it. The limp didn't ruin me. It *renamed* me.

You don't need a perfect resume to be called. You just need to stop hiding the limp. This is the beginning of living with a new name. It's the pivot point. Where the old name cracks. Where the striving fades. And a new strength begins to speak. We all wear name tags we didn't ask for.

So let me ask you:
What name tag have you been wearing?
Who gave it to you? And what if the name that matters most came after the break?

FROM GRABBER TO GRIT: WHEN PURPOSE RENAMES YOU

By sunrise, Jacob was filthy. His robes were soaked in sweat, matted with river mud, his muscles aching, his hip throbbing, his breath ragged. But he didn't let go.

He *couldn't*. Not until something changed. Not until he had a name for who he was becoming. And then it came:

"Your name will no longer be Jacob, but Israel, because you have struggled with God and with men — and have overcome."

This wasn't a clean "I've arrived" moment.
No spotlight.
No applause.
No trophy.

Jacob didn't emerge with arms raised in victory. He stood bent, limping, exhausted, gritting his way toward hope. And that's how purpose usually finds us.

Not in the podcast-ready quotes. Not in the curated highlight reel. But in the dust of the fight. In the ache. In the clarity that only comes through collapse. Purpose isn't proven by polish. It's revealed through perseverance. Jacob's new name didn't mean the wrestle was over. He still had to face Esau. Still had to walk into uncertainty. Still had to deal with the consequences of his past. Still had to lead a fractured, complicated family — and not just a family, but a generational enterprise. But something *had* shifted.

He wasn't walking for approval anymore.
He was walking with limp-earned clarity.

We often think finding purpose means discovering a dream job or grand calling. But purpose isn't your job title. It's not a moment. It's not a career ladder. It's your core identity. It's what you were *made* for.

How you live it out — that's your assignment. It shifts with seasons. But purpose is deeper. It doesn't change when your circumstances do. It's the thread that anchors you. To create. To multiply good. To bring order where there's chaos. To fill what's empty. To live intentionally in the image of the One who made you.

And for the fear-driven achiever — you've been sprinting for validation. But the limp slowed you down. And in the slowing, you found something speed never gave you: Direction. Clarity. Presence. Now, you move differently. You choose intentionally. You listen to what matters. You don't have to prove every step. In a world that rewards speed and spectacle, sometimes the quiet walk forward is the bravest thing you can do.

And for leaders? Your credibility doesn't come from never being knocked down. It comes from what you do *after*. Jacob wasn't disqualified by the limp. He was *distinguished* by it. The people you lead don't need your perfection. They need your presence. They need proof that the wrestle was real. And that purpose *survived it*. The limp isn't your weakness. It's your *credential*.

Jacob no longer walked as the one who grasped for blessing. He walked as the one renamed by pain, marked by transformation. The dirt on his robes was evidence of the fight. The limp was proof of the process. The name was a reminder: He didn't just survive. He *transformed*.

So let me ask:

Where are you still trying to look strong—
when the real strength is in your limp?

EMBRACING A NEW MINDSET: FROM DRIVEN TO DIRECTED

We've been taught to see breaking as failure. To bounce back. To push through. To overcome. But some stories rewrite the rules. Take Marvel actor Jeremy Renner —

After a devastating snowplow accident in 2023, most people assumed his action-hero days were over. Multiple fractures. Months of therapy. An uncertain future. But instead of disappearing, Renner did something rare: He let the world *see* the slow rebuild. Physical therapy. Emotional honesty. One painful step at a time. Still leading. Still fathering. Still showing up — not in spite of the pain, but *with* it. He didn't come back the same man. He came back more focused. More intentional. Less driven by status. More defined by substance.

That's what began to shift in me too. After surgery, I couldn't perform like I used to. Couldn't outwork the pain. Couldn't "bounce back" to normal. The metrics that used to define me — speed. Output. Flawless execution — no longer applied. At first, I fought it. Still tried to prove I was strong. Tried to outrun the reality of my injury. But my body said otherwise. And slowly, something deeper began to surface.

I started to listen.
To observe.
To move with intention instead of instinct.

Hustle without healing leads to collapse. But healing births a different kind of strength — quiet, grounded, and real. It didn't feel empowering at first. It felt like surrender. But over time, surrender became the gateway. I stopped rushing. Stopped proving. Started asking better questions:

What actually matters?
What's mine to carry?
What honors both purpose and recovery?

And the pressure that had defined me for years… lifted.

For the fear-driven achiever — you've been told that more is always better. That effort equals worth. That rest is weakness. But what if wisdom means walking with a limp — on purpose? What if the most powerful version of you isn't the fastest or the flashiest — but the one finally aligned with truth? This isn't a new hustle. It's a new walk.

And for leaders? Intensity can build momentum. But intention builds *legacy*. The most effective leaders aren't just fast. They're present. They've been through something. And they lead from *that*.

So I'll ask you:
Where are you leading fast when you should
be leading deep?

Direction is more powerful than speed — especially when you've been broken open. The mindset shift won't happen overnight. It's slow. Uneven. Messy. But one day, you wake up and realize… you're no longer living for the next thing. You're living from something deeper. And in those moments, Give yourself grace. Extend it to others. And that's where transformation begins to multiply.

> Where have you confused *motion* with *meaning*?
> And what would it look like to move with quiet, purposeful clarity instead?

A NAME WORTH LIMPING FOR THE PAIN DIDN'T DISQUALIFY YOU – IT REINTRODUCED YOU

Some scars don't fade. They follow you. Jacob left that riverside encounter with a blessing, a new name, and a limp. That limp wasn't a curse. It was a mark. Proof that something real had happened. Proof that he had stopped running. Proof that he had wrestled for his life… and lived. And for the rest of his days, it would remind him of who he now was.

It's easy to imagine that after that moment, everything clicked into place. But healing isn't instant. And identity doesn't settle overnight. It's forged through heat and pressure, shaped by surrender, held together by a vision of something deeper. Jacob walked away renamed, but not yet fully restored. He still had a past to face. Consequences to own. Relationships to mend. Habits to unlearn.

He had to *live* into the name "Israel."
Not just answer to it.
That's how it happens for us, too.

You survive something that should have undone you. Should have broken you. Should have ended your momentum… or your identity altogether. But somehow, you emerge. With less swagger… and more soul. You get handed a new name — maybe not audibly, but internally. And then comes the real work: learning how to live like it's true.

It's not a single decision.
It's a daily one.
It's not a state of being.
It's a state of *becoming*.

I remember looking in the mirror after surgery — and not recognizing the person staring back. The physical pain was starting to fade. But the internal questions? **They echoed**. I was no longer the person I had built my identity around: not the soldier. Not the performer. Not the strongest son, but the disabled one. Not the one who could outrun pain through discipline and perfect execution. There were no titles to fall back on. No stats to stand on. Just me — limping, healing, unsure… but new.

The limp taught me what the sprint never could. I started to listen differently. To trust slower timelines. To believe that worth doesn't come from force — it flows from identity. And maybe that's what Jacob realized too. That even in pain… even after failure… even limping into the unknown… he had been named by something deeper than what he had done. Your worth was never in the armor.

For the fear-driven achiever, you've spent years trying to earn approval, avoid weakness, and hide what hurts. You've lived with the pressure to be at 100% — as if that's what made you worthy. But you don't need a flawless resume to be called. You don't need to win every time to be seen. You don't need to hide the limp to lead.

Some of the actions you've taken, some of the patterns you've reinforced, have been with you for decades. Maybe they were built on a broken rule set — one you didn't even realize you were following. But now you have a choice. Whether you believe in divine blessing or simply hard-won growth, the truth is the same: you don't become who you are by winning every fight. You become who you are by refusing to let go — even when you're limping.

And leaders — you don't lead from perfection. You lead from permission. Sometimes the most powerful thing you can do is stop hiding the limp that tells the truth. Scars don't sabotage your influence. They *humanize* it. And your people? They'll see it. They'll trust it. Because when you lead from a place of authenticity — you're not leading from theory. You're leading from transformation.

What if the limp you've been hiding is
actually the name you've been growing into?

You might still be healing.
You might still be limping.

But you're *walking forward*.
And that's more powerful than you know.
Because the pain didn't disqualify you.

It reintroduced you.

YOUR GIANTS ARE LYING TO YOU

Chapter 4

WALKING WITH A LIMP

LEADING WITH A LIMP

You don't have to hide the cost of becoming...

When Jacob crossed back over the Jabbok River, he wasn't the same man who had fled years earlier. He walked differently now—literally.

The limp wasn't just a mark of injury. It was evidence of encounter. He had wrestled with God, been renamed, and blessed. But that blessing came with a cost.

And now, he had to lead with that limp.

That's where this part of the story begins—not in a tent, or on a battlefield, or behind a podium—but in the strange middle place.

The in-between space where transformation has occurred, and now you have to live with it.

For me, it looked like stepping out of a 30-bed rural hospital and into a nationally recognized pediatric health system with over 300 beds. On paper, it was a leap forward: more responsibility, more influence, and high-stakes environments—cardiac imaging in the OR, pandemic-era supply chain leadership, top-tier surgical teams. But I didn't walk in with a spring in my step. I walked in limping.

I was still recovering from the first hip surgery—learning my limits, flinching at each step, unsure what healing would really require. And yet, here I was, leading the very types of teams that had once helped rebuild me… while quietly navigating the limitations that surgery had left behind.

Truth Drop: The limp doesn't disqualify you. It qualifies you to lead from a deeper place.

At first, I tried to hide it. I moved slower, but made it look intentional. I was in pain, but framed it as recovery. I arrived early, stayed late, and carried the weight of proving I still belonged—even as my body whispered doubts I didn't want to say out loud:

> *Can I lead while limping?*
> *Will they follow someone who walks with pain?*
> *I look the part… but what if I don't feel it anymore?*

Then something began to shift. The limp made me slower—but slowness wasn't failure. It became attentiveness. I started noticing more. I asked better questions. I made room for nuance, for moments I used to rush past. I made more time for my staff. And I began to realize: slower isn't smaller. Wiser doesn't always look faster.

Ironically, I found myself leading from the same places that had once rebuilt me—the OR, the imaging suite, physical therapy sessions. It was poetic. But it wasn't painless. There were days I sat during meetings because standing hurt. Moments I paused mid-walk, hiding the hitch in my stride behind a clipboard, an iPad, or a forced conversation. I carried the responsibility of leadership and the weight of limitation at the same time. And I wasn't always sure how long I could keep doing both. The fear-driven achiever in me screamed: *If you slow down, you'll fail.*

And then the quiet signals started again—deep aches, twinges I couldn't ignore, a creeping sense that healing had stalled. It was all too familiar. I told myself it was normal recovery. I kept pushing forward—because that's what we do, right? Leaders don't complain. Achievers don't pause. Strong people don't admit they're still hurting—especially not when everyone else thinks you're better.

But the truth was this: my healing wasn't finished. And the limp wasn't just a symbol of what I'd survived—it was a preview of what was still unresolved.

For the fear-driven achiever, hear this: You're not broken just because you're not done healing. You're not failing just because you're moving slower. You're learning to lead with honesty—and that's a rare strength.

And for every leader: you don't have to hide the cost of becoming. People don't need you to be pain-free. They need you to be present. To be real. To show up limping and still leading. The limp may slow you down—but it makes you human. It makes you approachable. And it gives others permission to drop their armor too.

Maybe your limp isn't in your stride. Maybe it's in your story. Your nervous system. Your soul. Whatever it is—don't discount it. That's where your wisdom is being formed. Don't believe the lie your giant keeps whispering—that you have to lead like nothing's changed when everything has.

THE WEIGHT OF THE INVISIBLE

Pain doesn't have to be visible to be real. Some wounds leave marks. Others just leave weight. That's the paradox of invisible pain. The world sees recovery—but your soul knows better. You're standing. You're functioning. You're even excelling. But inside, you're limping just to make it through the day.

That's what those months felt like for me. I was leading a high-performing surgical services team at one of the most respected pediatric hospitals in the region. We were solving complex problems at scale. Innovating. Delivering. From the outside, everything looked strong. But underneath, the pain had returned. There was no cast. No crutch. No visible sign of injury. But my hip throbbed quietly with every step.

And worse than the physical pain… was the emotional weight of pretending it wasn't there. Of fearing it would grow into something worse. Of knowing that, eventually, it would crack the image I'd worked so hard to maintain.

Just because the world can't see your limp doesn't mean you're not leading with it. I remember walking into morning huddles—iPad in hand, phone holstered, voice steady—while second-guessing every step. I'd sit through meetings, subtly shifting in my chair, trying to relieve the ache without revealing it.

And I told myself:

*If I just perform well enough, maybe I'll forget the pain...
or at least they won't see it.*

But pain doesn't stay hidden. It seeps into everything: Your decisions. Your presence. Your patience. Your relationships. Your waking hours... and your sleeping ones. It doesn't just affect your body. It shapes how you show up—at work, at home, with the people you love.

And the hardest part?
The silence.

Because once people see you "back at it," they assume the story's over. You survived. You're fine now. Right? But "back to normal" is a myth when you've been broken open.

For the high-functioning, fear-driven achiever— you can be excellent at what you do... and still carry pain no one sees. And the longer you go without naming it, the heavier it gets. The pressure builds. The silence becomes bondage. And the cycle repeats.

I felt guilty for needing breaks. Guilty for sitting when others stood. Guilty for needing help when I had always prided myself on never needing anything. It's a strange kind of shame—the kind that forms when you look capable but feel fractured. And in a culture where speed equals strength and burnout is worn like a badge of honor, asking for margin feels like weakness.

That's what made it so hard to admit I wasn't okay.
And hadn't been for a long time.

Jacob knew this paradox too. Yes, he had been renamed. Yes, he had survived the night. But he still had to limp back into camp—into family, into legacy, into the unknown—with a wound that never fully healed. He still had to face Esau. Still had to provide. Still had to lead change… while everyone expected him to function like nothing had happened.

That's what most people will never understand — unless they've lived it. Healing doesn't erase the expectation to keep performing. For leaders, leadership doesn't pause just because your body or heart is hurting. But that doesn't mean you have to fake strength to maintain trust. You don't have to hide what was never meant to be carried alone. And even if you're not in a formal leadership role—if you're a parent, a teacher, a caregiver, a friend—if others rely on you—you know this weight too.

Here's the truth: You can't outwork invisible pain. You can only name it, honor it, and begin to listen to what it's trying to teach you. So pause here for a moment: What weight are you carrying that no one sees? And what might change if you finally named it?

WHEN THE PACE CHANGES, SO DOES THE PERSPECTIVE

Slow doesn't mean stuck. It means you're seeing more. Life used to feel like a sprint. Move fast. Keep up. Outwork the pain. Double down and get there before anyone notices you're struggling. You could rest — briefly — once the task was done, once the next milestone was checked. Then back to motion.

But after the injury, after everything that followed, that kind of pace wasn't an option anymore. The sprint had to stop. And at first? It felt like failure. Like falling behind. Like watching everyone else race ahead while you sat still. Legs sore. Calendar thinning. Calling paused. Purpose fading. But eventually, I started to see something else.

When you stop rushing, you start noticing. *Urgency isn't the same as clarity.* In the slow-down, I began to pay attention in ways I hadn't before. I noticed how people moved. I picked up on what others missed. I started asking new questions—not just "What's the problem?" but "What's the pattern?" I stopped treating symptoms and started tracing roots. The pause created margin. The margin created insight. And insight birthed clarity.

At work, I saw team dynamics I used to miss. I noticed tension before it boiled over. I picked up on body language, long silences, the sighs behind the smiles. I understood the

"when,"
the "where,"
and the "why"
—not just the "what."

And in life? I realized how deeply my identity had been tethered to motion. Without constant forward progress, I didn't know how to measure my value.

I had confused velocity with meaning. Tied my sense of worth to productivity. And lost the clarity that comes with being grounded in purpose. Before the injury, I moved fast because I thought I had to. After the injury, I moved slow because I had no choice. But somewhere in between… I found vision.

Jacob limped after the wrestle, but it didn't stop him from leading. If anything, it gave him something most leaders never find: clarity. He could no longer outrun discomfort, so he had to face it. And in facing it, he saw everything differently—his family. His legacy. His responsibility. His own role in what came next. And what he saw shaped generations to come.

For the fear-driven achiever, hear this: you're not behind just because you're moving slower. You're becoming someone who sees differently. And that's the beginning of wisdom. Your moment of clarity isn't late — it's on time. Not every breakthrough happens fast. And some of the best ones don't.

And leaders? Speed is useful. But clarity is sustainable. Some of your most effective decisions won't come from adrenaline or urgency. They'll come from a quiet, slow-down gut check that no one else sees but you. Not from reaction. But from response. Not noise first—but listening first.

World renowned tennis player Naomi Osaka walked away from a major tournament to protect her mental health. The world didn't lose respect for her. They stood in awe as she reclaimed her name, her pace, her power. *Stepping back isn't weakness. It's strategy.*

For me, slowing down didn't mean sitting out. It meant seeing differently. I caught inefficiencies others rushed past. I picked up emotional cues before they became disengagement. I led less with adrenaline and more with awareness. And over time, something surprising happened: I stopped wasting time. I started feeling it again. For anyone walking through grief, burnout, caregiving, or long-term recovery—sometimes slowing down isn't a luxury. It's survival.

So let me ask: Where in your life have you mistaken speed for strength? And what might you start to see… if you moved a little slower?

There's a saying I learned in the Army:
"Slow is smooth. Smooth is fast."

But when you're wired like a fear-driven achiever, speed becomes a form of self-preservation. If you move fast enough, maybe you won't have to repeat anything. And if you never have to repeat anything, maybe you won't feel like a failure.

But what if we adopted a different rhythm? What if we trusted the pace of smooth—and the clarity that comes when we're no longer driven by fear?

REDEFINING STRENGTH

What if the strongest thing you can do… is let someone else carry it for a while? In high school, I was voted "Most Dependable." It followed me. Into the Army. Into my first jobs. Into hospital leadership. Into every room where people expected me to show up, deliver, and never drop the ball. I had made an internal contract with myself early on: If I say I'll do it—I will. Period.

I was the one others could count on. The one who didn't flinch under pressure. The one who pushed through. Flawless execution, every time. And that kind of identity gets reinforced quickly. Especially when it works.

Until it doesn't.

After my first surgery, I tried to return to form. I showed up like I always had—determined to prove I still had it, even with a hip that didn't work the way it used to. But my body didn't agree. Some days I couldn't lift what needed lifting. Some days I needed to sit while my team stood. Some days I'd walk into a meeting and feel breathless—not from exertion, but from the emotional toll of admitting: I can't do what I used to do. Even when I doubled down, it failed me. And it cost more than what I gained. And then came the shame. The disappointment. The unraveling of the story I'd told myself for years.

Strength doesn't mean doing it all. It means knowing when to ask for help. At first, I resisted. I told myself it was temporary. If I just pushed harder, I'd bounce back. But I wasn't bouncing. I was breaking. And for the first time in a long time… I couldn't power through it. The narrative I'd built my identity on—

>Be the rock.
>Be the one.
>Be the answer.
>Double down.
>Deliver flawlessly—
>…was unraveling.
>And I didn't know who I was without it.

But something unexpected began to shift. I didn't need to be the subject matter expert anymore. I needed to empower the experts around me. I started stepping back—not out of apathy, but out of trust. I moved from execution to elevation. From being the one who lifted… to building the team that could lift together.

And for the fear-driven achiever? You don't have to be the strongest one in the room. You just have to be present enough to listen, to lead, to lift others up. To notice the strengths they don't see in themselves. To draw out purpose in their story. To help them rise into the work they're called to. There's a kind of strength that doesn't come from domination or performance. It comes from permission. Creating space. Sharing weight. Letting someone else rise.

Leadership doesn't always mean pushing through. Sometimes it means stepping aside—just long enough for someone else to step forward. And watching them grow. Stepping back isn't stepping down. It's making room. Think about a football coach—they're not on the field next to the quarterback or linemen. They're on the sidelines. Coaching. Equipping. Empowering others to play their part.

Jacob didn't get a polished ending. He got a limp. A new name. A fractured family. And a legacy to carry. But he still walked forward—imperfect, renamed, and present. He blessed his children. Made peace with Esau. And he learned how to walk while leaning on others. Not with the same physical power…but with deeper presence. *The limp didn't disqualify him. It refined him.*

For me, that refinement rewrote everything I thought I knew about strength. I had spent years chasing a scoreboard that was never truly mine. But the limp… The limits… The letting go…they forced a question I could no longer ignore:

What if I've been measuring the wrong things all along?

Strength used to mean no weakness. No pause. No help needed. Now? Strength looks like this: asking for what you need. Empowering the people around you. Listening more than directing. Leading from presence—not performance. And even if you're not managing a team—if you're raising kids, running a household, caregiving, or carrying invisible weight—you've probably worn this kind of armor too.

So here's the question: What version of strength have you been trying to live up to? And what might change if you finally let it go?

NAMING THE REAL GIANT

It was never just the limp. It was the lie I believed about it. It took me years to recognize the real breaking point. Not the surgery. Not the pain. Not even the collapse.

The real shattering moment wasn't physical. It was psychological. It was the illusion I had been living under all along. For years, I leaned in harder. I doubled down. If I just worked more, planned better, stayed in control—I could hold it all together. The fear-driven achiever inside me whispered:

> **You can't fail.**
> **You mustn't stop.**
> **If you pause, it all falls apart.**

I didn't just hear that lie. I believed it. I built my life around it. Fear had become my operating system. And like any well-disguised virus, it didn't roar. It whispered.

Then came the trifecta: ten years of chronic pain. A house remodel during a pandemic—laying down 3,000 square feet of laminate flooring with a body already falling apart. And finally, the moment it all snapped. Pain surged like lightning. I could barely walk. Every step toward the OR felt like betrayal—
>of my body,
>my expectations,
>my identity.

Desperate, I went to the doctor. He glanced at the x-rays and said, *"It's arthritis. You're too young for a hip replacement. You'll have to wait."* He meant well. But what I heard was:

>**Your pain isn't real.**
>**There's no solution.**
>**This is your life now.**

I left that office not just hurting—but hopeless. And hope deferred makes the heart sick. That night, as the sun disappeared behind the trees and the house grew still, the whisper returned. Only this time, it wasn't subtle.

>*If I can't walk, how can I work?*
>*If I can't work, how can I provide?*
>*If I can't provide, how can I have a family?*
>*If I can't bounce my future child on my knee without being in pain, am I even a man anymore?*

For you, the questions may sound different:
>*Am I even a woman worth trusting anymore?*
>*Am I even a person who matters, if I can't do what I used to do?*
>*If I can't fulfill my calling… does my life still have purpose?*

They weren't just questions. They were accusations. Each one a blow. Each one an echo. Each one aimed at the image I had built—and feared I was losing. That was the night the real giant spoke. Not the limp. Not the pain. But the fear behind them. The shame that said:

You're only as valuable as your capacity.
And if you lose that… you lose everything.
You have no purpose.

The loudest giants don't always roar. Sometimes, they whisper. I thought I had made peace with the limp. But I hadn't even named the thing behind it. I wasn't just afraid of being weak. I was afraid of being worthless. We talk about burnout. But we don't always talk about the silent breakdown that happens when fear and performance become your only compass. When you're not just tired…you're unraveling. But no one sees it—because from the outside, you still look like you have it all together.

That's what nearly took me out. Not the injury. But the collapse of identity. And in that shadowed room, I felt something I hadn't allowed myself to feel in years: I didn't want to go on. I had no plan. But I had crossed into dangerous emotional terrain. And if you've ever been there, you know—it's not about logic. It's about despair. The kind that sinks into your bones and tells you you'll never matter again. Not to your family. Not to your calling. Not to the world.

Crushed.
Unseen.
Done.

And then… the phone rang.
A friend.
A check-in.

A mercy I didn't even know I needed. I answered. And I told him everything. The fear. The shame. The unraveling. The real identity behind the limp. And something shifted. Not because I was fixed. But because—for the first time—I was real. The next morning, I made the appointment. This time, I didn't walk in trying to prove I was strong. I walked in fighting for the truth.

For the fear-driven achiever: you can serve fear for a long time and call it discipline. But eventually… **The voice you obey will reveal the name of the giant you've been bowing to.** And for leaders? You don't lead well by hiding your unraveling. You lead well by recognizing the whisper—and choosing to fight back.

So let me ask you: **What lie have you been listening to that's shaping how you lead, live, or see yourself?** And what would it take… to finally call it what it really is?

THE LONG GAME OF HEALING

You don't have to be all better to begin again. Healing doesn't make headlines. It rarely comes with a grand moment of arrival. **It comes on Tuesdays.**

The quiet, unremarkable kind of day—where nothing feels significant, except your decision to keep going.

After the collapse, after the whispering giant, after the phone call that pulled me back from the edge… came the cost. Choosing to fight wasn't free. It meant facing the need for another surgery. Eight more weeks of recovery. More physical therapy. More bills. More pain. More dependence. I'd need help getting up the stairs. Help carrying groceries. Help covering meetings I could no longer attend. I had to relinquish control—not because I wanted to, but because I had to.

At the pediatric hospital, my team still needed leadership. But I couldn't be physically present. That meant practicing one of the hardest leadership disciplines I've ever had to learn: Letting go… without dropping the mission. I didn't just create a backup plan. I equipped my people. I empowered them to lead, to trust their own instincts, to stop looking to me for every cue—and instead, to discover their own sense of purpose in the work we shared.

And at the very same time, I was learning to be led. In a rehab room full of resistance bands and balance boards, I traded my role as leader for the role of patient. My physical therapist became my coach. My challenger. My accountability partner. I wasn't calling the shots anymore. I was learning to follow directions, to push through discomfort, to rest when instructed, and to trust someone else with my healing.

There was no white-knuckling it. No doubling down. No powering through. Only presence. Only practice. Only process. It was humbling. And deeply humanizing. Pain slowed me down, but in that stillness… I began to see what I'd missed. Team dynamics that had gone unnoticed. Emotional undercurrents I used to override. Quiet strengths in others that had gone unspoken.

My injury became a magnifying lens. It didn't just show me what hurt. It showed me what mattered. It brought clarity—not just for the moment I was in, but for how I wanted to lead going forward. Because healing isn't just a physical process. It's a leadership discipline. It's the courage to hand off. To be coached. To step back—not because you're less, but because you're preparing the way forward. And hear this: the moment you become the one being coached… isn't a sign of weakness. It's the beginning of deeper strength.

A NEW LEASE ON LIFE

Healing doesn't erase the past—but it can redefine the future. My second surgery felt different. Same hospital setting. Same preop process. But the moment I woke up, I knew. The pain was gone. Not all the soreness. Not full range of motion yet. But the deep pain—the kind that had settled into my bones, that made every step a calculation, that shadowed every single day—it was just… gone.

I lay there in the recovery room, blinking through anesthesia, holding still. Not from fear. But from awe.

Is this what relief feels like?

I'd lived with pain for so long that I had forgotten what it felt like to move without guarding. But now, for the first time in over a decade, I wasn't fighting against my body. I was moving with it.

Healing didn't just restore what was broken.
It reconnected me to myself.

Later, I read the surgical notes. A donor graft had been used—human tissue, a piece of someone else's life now woven into mine. A stranger's final gift had become my new beginning. Someone's ending became my rebirth. I didn't just heal from something. I healed with something—something sacred, something shared. Whether that donor's family ever knew it or not, their loved one's legacy now walks with me. Their generosity gave me more than physical repair—it gave me forward motion.

You are not the same person on the other side of healing. You don't just carry recovery. You carry responsibility. The gift was given. What will you do with it? Your wholeness might just be someone else's hope. And for the fear-driven achiever: You don't have to earn your second chance. Sometimes grace arrives as a gift you could never orchestrate. And healing becomes the way you say thank you.

Recovery wasn't passive. I showed up. I trained. I stretched. I rebuilt. Some days I shook. Some days I swore. Every day I sweat. But I kept moving. Not to get back to who I used to be—but to become who I was always meant to be. This wasn't just healing. It was transformation.

Eventually, the limp faded. There were days I didn't notice it. Then weeks. Then months. Until one day, I caught myself walking across a parking lot—no hitch. No flinch. No thought. No limp. Just life again. But this time, fuller. More grounded. More present. That's when I knew: this wasn't a return to how things were.

This was a new story beginning.

No, you may not get back the time pain stole. For me, it was over a decade. But you can reclaim what fear tried to take. You can rebuild your rhythm. You can replant what was lost—this time, in the right soil. This time, with roots. This is what healing makes possible. You're allowed to begin again. And what if that moment you thought was the end…was actually the beginning?

SCARS THAT SPEAK

The scars remain. Not just the ones beneath the skin — hidden from view — but the ones I carried in the rhythm of my steps, in the patience I learned, in the way I started listening differently.

For years, I tried to outrun the damage. Tried to overcompensate. Tried to pretend the limp wasn't there. I doubled down. I powered through. But now? I don't need to. Because I've come to understand — the scar isn't the end of the story. It's the punctuation mark that proves I survived the middle.

When I woke up in the recovery room after the second surgery, groggy but alert, I asked what had happened. The team explained they had replaced my labrum with a donated human allograft. A gift from someone I would never know. Someone whose final act in this life became the beginning of something new in mine. Their generosity gave me a future. And almost immediately… I noticed something. The pain that had defined nearly a decade of my life was gone. Yes, there were six fresh surgical incisions on my hip. But the deep, bone-aching pain? Vanished.

I declined the pain meds at first—I knew they'd make me sick. The nurse pushed. I caved. Sure enough—I was sick. But I was right. And I knew something else, too: this pain wasn't suffering. This was healing. Physical therapy started quickly, and this time, it felt different. Less than 10 days post-op, I was cleared to begin weaning off crutches. A far cry from the six-week recovery required after the first surgery.

The limp didn't return. The pain stayed gone. And even now—it hasn't come back. I still stretch. I still train. I still strengthen. But I'm not limping through life anymore. That chapter is closed. That identity has expired.

Jacob walked away from the Jabbok with a limp. But he walked forward—into his family, into his legacy, into his future. He didn't go back to who he was before. He stepped boldly into who he was always meant to be. So did I. I didn't return to work the same. I walked slower. I sat more. I asked better questions. I listened for what wasn't being said.

My limp made me less interested in being impressive—and more determined to be present. There were days that felt like a loss. But most days… it felt like clarity.

Here's the truth:
We all limp. Some of us just have the gift of knowing it. And when you stop hiding the scar, you start discovering something powerful:

Your story becomes someone else's permission to hope.

That's why I write.
That's why I lead the way I do.
Not because I have it all figured out.

But because I've been knocked down, broken open—and still chose to rise…with a scar that now speaks louder than the hustle ever could.

You don't need to hide the scar. It might be the only thing someone else needs to see—to believe they can heal too.

The limp was gone.
For the first time in a decade, I walked steady.
No catching pain.
No crooked stride.

Just movement.
Just freedom.
Just hope.

But healing—when pain has been your closest companion—can leave a strange silence. And in that silence, I listened. Not for the ache. But for the absence of it. And that's when I heard it again:

A whisper.
Faint.
Familiar.

What if this doesn't last?
What if the pain comes back?
What if you fall into old patterns again?

I turned instinctively to the corner of my bedroom—the same corner where everything had collapsed months before. Nothing was there. But something was.

A presence.
A weight.
Not pain.
Not failure.

Something I couldn't see, but could feel—recognized only by the echo of its whisper.

The limp was gone.

And the shadow, too, had lost its hold.

Chapter 5

FACING GOLIATH – FEAR, COURAGE, AND DESTINY COLLIDE

THE ECHO OF THE GIANT'S ROAR

Healing doesn't silence the echo. It teaches you what not to believe.

The whispers didn't vanish after healing. They got smarter. Quieter. Once the limp faded, the voice of fear didn't roar. It murmured.

You're not out of the woods. You'll never be fully back.
Don't get too confident. It could all fall apart.
Who you are will fail.

That's the trap. When fear can't grip your body, it grips your mind. It doesn't shout. It hisses. And if you're not careful, the whisper fades into the background—so constant you mistake it for truth.

YOUR GIANTS ARE LYING TO YOU

That's exactly how Goliath, the Philistine champion, worked. He never had to throw a spear. He just had to speak. For forty days—morning and evening—he shouted across the valley. And Israel froze. A nation paralyzed not by violence, but by a voice. Strong men stood still. Not because they were wounded… but because they were convinced.

Goliath knew the secret: If you control someone's fear, you don't need to touch their body. You can steal their courage. You can rewrite their identity. You can hold their future hostage. The text doesn't say the warriors were defeated in battle. They were defeated in imagination.

That's the anatomy of a giant. It starts as a whisper. Echoes into a roar. Convinces you the outcome is already written—that defeat is inevitable. You know that feeling. You're capable. You've accomplished a lot. Maybe even admired. But when it gets quiet, the echo returns.

If you fail now, it's over.
This was just a fluke.
They're going to find out you don't belong here.

That's not your voice. It's the echo of a giant's roar—just dressed up in your tone. And that's where David steps in, a young shepherd from Bethlehem (1 Samuel 17).

A teenager with a delivery order for his older brothers and, a faithful heart walks into a camp full of frozen men. Confident warriors… paralyzed, including his own brothers. He hears the same taunt. He sees the same threat.

But where everyone else hears a roar and freezes—David hears a lie and burns.

This isn't just a story about courage. It's a story about clarity. Because the roar wasn't just a physical threat. It was generational. It challenged Israel's future. It questioned God's promise. It echoed an ancient whisper: *"Did God really say…?"* And maybe that's what's happening in your story too.

You've silenced the limp, but not the lie. You've healed the body, but the whisper still finds you in the dark. Fear doesn't always shout on the battlefield. Sometimes it speaks loudest in the silence before the fight. In the quiet. In the night. But what if the whisper is wrong? What if the roar is fear—inflated but empty? What if the giant's voice isn't your verdict—but your invitation?

David didn't win by yelling louder. He won because he rejected the terms and conditions that fear tried to sell him. He stood in the same valley. He heard the same roar. But he chose to believe a different voice.

That's the invitation for leaders too. You don't have to out-shout the noise. You just have to stop agreeing with the lie. You have to reframe the terms. You have to choose clarity.

So ask yourself honestly:

Where are you still hearing the roar?

And what would it mean to reject its terms and conditions?

Because sometimes, the bravest thing you'll ever do… is stop letting fear do the talking. You don't need to roar to be free. You just need to stop agreeing with the lie.

WHAT GIANTS LOOK LIKE TODAY

The lie isn't always loud. Sometimes it's just familiar. Giants don't always wear armor. They don't tower nine feet tall or shout across a battlefield. But they still show up—in your calendar, in your childhood, in your culture. They live in your inbox, your expectations, your social media scroll. They whisper through legacy. They echo through family dynamics. They hide behind the pressure to keep climbing, keep proving, keep hustling—to execute with flawless precision.

I used to think giants would be easy to spot. But the ones that shaped me? They never raised their voices. They just handed me a script. And I followed it. Be the oldest. Be the responsible one. Make sure it works. Don't let anyone down. My family had shifted industries—from artisan bookbinders into something new after books went digital instead of paper. But the names on the ledger weren't the only thing passed down. The silent rules came too. If you're not building something… If you're not carrying the weight… Then who even are you?

I wasn't told to lead. I was expected to. And like so many fear-driven achievers, I mistook pressure for purpose. I confused what I was doing with who I was becoming. I didn't know I was living under a giant…because the whisper felt normal.

David's story isn't just ancient poetry. It's a mirror. When the prophet Samuel came to anoint the next king of Israel, Jesse didn't even invite David, his youngest son, to the ceremony. Not because he hated him—but because he couldn't see it. To Jesse, David was just a shepherd. Useful, but ordinary. The youngest? Not a chance. The next king? Surely it had to be someone taller. Older. Obvious.

Sound familiar? We don't always dismiss ourselves. Sometimes, we've just never been seen as more than what we've always done. It's the same with job applications. Artificial intelligence and recruiters look at your résumé and assume that what you've done…is all you want to do. So you get recruited again and again for the same role you're trying to outgrow. The system locks you into the cycle. The giant keeps handing you the same script.

But today's giants aren't made of bronze. They're built from assumptions. They're forged in silence. They're passed down as invisible rules. Don't dream too big. Stick to what works. Prove your worth. Don't mess it up. Stay in your lane.

David didn't just fight Goliath—he broke a generational expectation. Because Jesse, like so many of us, could only see what he knew. He couldn't imagine what was possible. That's the trap. If your father couldn't imagine it… If your boss has never seen it… If your culture doesn't reward it… If your likes on social media don't reflect it… You start believing it isn't real.

But here's the truth: What your giant says doesn't define you. What your family couldn't see doesn't limit you. What culture handed you isn't the end of your story. What doesn't get likes doesn't make it any less true. You've got to name the giant. Not to make it smaller—but to make it visible. So pause here for a moment.

- What have you inherited that feels like truth but might actually be a lie?
- Whose voice shaped your internal script?
- What are you still trying to prove—and to whom?

And if you're leading others, ask yourself this: Are the scripts you've inherited still serving the people you lead — or just protecting the system you came from?

Naming the giant is the first act of defiance. Until you do, it still gets to hold the pen. It still writes your story. You didn't choose the script. But you get to choose whether to keep reading from it.

THE DECISION TO STEP FORWARD

Courage doesn't begin with confidence. It begins with refusal. David didn't just fight Goliath. He stepped forward — while everyone else stayed frozen. Same threat. Same battlefield. Same roar. But something in him said, "This doesn't get the final word." That's the weight of a single decision. It draws a line. What was can no longer be. It doesn't always look epic.

Sometimes it looks like a teenager with bread in one hand and clarity in the other. Sometimes it looks like someone sitting in a quiet room, whispering to themselves, *"I can't keep living like this."* No applause. No spotlight. No medals. Just a quiet pivot. A shift in posture. A moment where something inside refuses to stay paralyzed.

The story didn't change because the giant disappeared. It changed because someone moved. That's the hinge point for the fear-driven achiever. Not the outcome—the decision. We assume transformation happens in the win. But most of it happens in the pivot. That internal break from the lie.

> The moment you stop agreeing with fear.
> The moment you whisper, "No more."
> The moment you stop performing for survival—
> and start showing up for truth.

For me, that moment wasn't flashy. But it was final. It came in a conversation I nearly avoided. A truth I almost swallowed. A quiet realization that pretending everything was fine was costing me too much. That's the cost of the call. You don't get guarantees. You don't get standing ovations. What you get is risk.

David knew it.

If he failed, Israel lost everything. But he also knew no one else was moving. And the price of staying stuck was higher than the risk of stepping in. That's what every fear-driven achiever has to face.

You can double down to protect the image— or step forward to protect something deeper. Fear-driven action is loud. It rushes to silence doubt.

> But purpose-driven courage?
> It doesn't have to shout.
> It just has to be clear.

David didn't step forward to prove anything. He stepped forward because the giant was mocking what he was made to protect: Identity. Purpose. Future. Legacy. And maybe that's where you are. You've heard the roar. You've lived the script. You know the stakes. And now, you're standing at the edge of a decision.

> Will you keep rehearsing the fear?
> Or will you step forward—
> even if your voice shakes and your hands tremble?

Because here's the deeper truth: One person's decision to move can shift the emotional climate of a team, a family, a culture, a generation. It only takes one voice to break the spell. And for all of us—whether we lead hundreds or are just trying to lead ourselves—every transformation begins with a choice. Not always visible. But always decisive. But don't miss this: The decision alone isn't the victory. It's the beginning.

Before David walked to the valley floor, he had to gather stones. He had to prepare. **So will you.**

THE WEIGHT OF THE DECISION

Some fights aren't just about survival. They're about freedom. David didn't volunteer to die. He volunteered to fight— because someone had to. He saw the valley for what it was: Not just a battlefield, but a crossroads. This wasn't only about him. It was about a nation. A future. A people's freedom.

He didn't step forward to prove his strength. He stepped forward to declare: **"The giant doesn't get to define us."** That's when a decision becomes non-negotiable—when the fear of staying stuck outweighs the fear of stepping forward. It doesn't mean the fear disappears. It just means something else gets louder. Purpose. Conviction. Legacy.

And in that moment, your life starts to echo something older. Something ancient. **Liberty or death.** Not just dramatic words for a revolutionary. *A declaration.* Some moments demand action—not because you're fearless, but because the cost of silence is too high. I know that moment. I lived it.

My second hip surgery wasn't just a medical choice. It was a turning point. After the first failed operation, part of me wanted to quit. To settle. To survive. But then came the verdict: The damage was worse. No guarantees this time. And in that moment, I had a choice—Stay stuck? Or fight again? Not just for mobility. But for meaning.

I chose to fight. Not to prove I was unbreakable, but to reclaim the purpose I was born to live:
To create.
To lead.
To move through the world unshackled by fear.

There's a difference between doubling down… and deciding to fight. Doubling down is fear's survival strategy, it says:

Don't slow down.
Don't show weakness.
Execute flawlessly.
Keep the mask on.

It's about image.
Perfection.
Pleasing the system.

But deciding to fight? That's about protecting your future. And the future of those who come after you. That's where freedom lives. Not in applause. Not in titles. Not in polished branding. But in the deep resolve to live as someone who builds, heals, risks, and leads—no longer controlled by the giant's voice. And when you live that way—others notice. Not just your strength, but your freedom. And your freedom gives them permission to pursue theirs.

So pause for a moment.
- Where in your life have you been doubling down instead of deciding to fight?

- What are you protecting—your image or your purpose?

- What might change if you fought for freedom, not perfection?

There's always a cost.

If David had stayed silent, the nation would've paid. If I had stayed silent, part of me would still be trapped behind pain and pretense. And if you stay silent— what's the cost in your story? Not just the cost of inaction, but of imagination. What is fear keeping you from building, from saying, from believing, from becoming?

That's why the decision isn't the end. It's just the crack in the illusion. The rupture in the silence. Even gathering your stones—that quiet preparation—is part of the story too. You don't have to have the battle figured out. You just have to be willing to act. Before David faced the giant, he gathered his stones. Before you step into your next valley, you will too.

WHEN THE WEAPONS CHANGE

What was meant to break you can become what builds others. David didn't win the battle with the giant's sword. But he finished it with one. That matters.

He brought Goliath down with a sling and a stone—the tools he had trained with in solitude. But when he crossed the field, he picked up the very weapon meant to destroy him. He lifted it as a declaration:

This doesn't belong to fear anymore.

It wasn't just a kill. It was a reframe. Because when David raised that sword, he didn't just end a threat. He transformed what once terrified others into a tool of victory.

In that moment, something shifted. The strong men who had stood still in fear suddenly surged forward. They remembered who they were. That's what redemption looks like. Not erasing the past—but reclaiming it.

I've come to see my own scars that way. Not as shameful. Not as something to hide. But as spiritual inventory. Visible reminders that pain, when held with wisdom, becomes purpose. I didn't choose the injury. Didn't ask for the setback. But somewhere along the way, those moments became how I learned to lead. Not because they made me impressive—but because they made me human.

I know what it's like to lose strength. To stare at a ceiling tile and wonder if your best days are behind you. To walk into a room and want to hide the limp—physical or otherwise. To carry the shame of having to mask what once made you feel powerful. But those moments gave me something deeper than resilience.

They gave me eyes.

Eyes to see the quiet fighters. The ones carrying invisible battles. The ones who lead without volume. The ones who've already made peace with their scars. And it changed the way I lead. Because when your wounds become tools of compassion, you stop posturing. You start building trust. You stop leading through control. And begin leading with presence. With authority born not from performance, but from experience.

The sling and the stones — those matter too. They represent the preparation. The practice. The faith. The courage to act when no one is watching. David didn't throw those away just because he picked up a sword. And neither should we. Because the goal isn't to upgrade weapons. It's to remember what made the breakthrough possible in the first place.

> God didn't need a sword.
> He used what David already carried.
> And that's true for you too.

You've likely been shaped by some kind of wound—physical, emotional, generational. But that doesn't mean the wound gets the last word. It may just become your sharpest tool. Not because of the pain—but because of the purpose that followed.

So ask yourself:

- What once threatened you?

- What name, moment, or memory tried to define your limits?

Now consider:
- Could that become part of your toolkit?

- Could it be what makes you the kind of leader who sees others more clearly?

Because in a culture obsessed with shiny swords and sharp hashtags, what the world needs now are leaders who still carry stones. Your wounds don't disqualify you. They prepare you.

THE ECHO AFTER THE ROAR

Just because the giant fell doesn't mean the voice vanished. The battlefield was silent. The giant was gone. But the echo remained. That's the part nobody talks about. The roar may have stopped—but its residue still lingers.

Fear doesn't always leave when the fight ends. Sometimes it stays behind like smoke after fire—not as a threat, but as memory. A faint vibration of who you used to be. That's what I noticed after surgery. The hip had been repaired. The pain was gone. But I still walked like I was broken. Not every step—but enough. Enough to reveal that the echo hadn't left. It had just changed form.

Be careful.

Play it safe.

Don't expect too much.

If it gets tough, double down.

That's the strange part of healing.

You can be physically restored—but still haunted by what used to hurt you. I remember walking down a fluorescent-lit hallway during an inventory. Boxes in hand. Empty air. No pain—but I caught myself limping anyway. Not from injury. From habit. That's when it hit me:

Healing isn't just physical.
It's mental.
Emotional.
Spiritual.

It requires great intentionality. And sometimes, it starts when someone sees you differently.

A nurse I barely knew passed me in the supply room. She nodded and said quietly, "I'm glad to see you're back. I'd wondered what happened to you." That's all it took. Her words became louder than the echo—not because she shouted, but because she noticed. Sometimes all it takes is to be seen in a new way to start believing a new story.

David had a moment like that too. After Goliath fell, he wasn't just "the kid with the sling" anymore. The shepherd boy who was supposed to stay in the fields—now stood in a new role. But nothing essential about him had changed. The shepherd didn't disappear. The musician didn't disappear. But those parts of him now had purpose.

David didn't lead because he won. He led because he stayed faithful—long enough for others to finally see it. That's how identity shifts. Not just through outcomes… but through echoes. The old echo says:

You're still not enough.
Don't let them down.
Stay small.
Stay safe.

But there's another kind of echo too. The whisper of courage. The moment someone sees you whole. The subtle invitation to walk like you're already free. Because most of us aren't still fighting giants. We're living in the quiet after. And in that hush, you get to choose what voice you follow.

- What echoes are still shaping how you move through the world today?
- What old warnings still whisper when you try to dream again?

You're not imagining them. But you don't have to obey them either. The echo is real—but it isn't true.

THE QUIET VOICE

Not all voices are loud. But some are true. The roar has faded. The echo has quieted. And now something else begins to rise. Not noise. Not fear. A voice you almost forgot how to hear. It doesn't demand. It doesn't shame. It doesn't push or manipulate. It builds. It invites.

It's the quiet voice of purpose. The voice that doesn't shout threats—but whispers reminders:

This is who you are.
This is what you were made for.
Create. Build. Bless. Steward.

It was always there—you just couldn't hear it over fear's performance. That's the shift. Fear shouts. Purpose whispers. And in the aftermath of healing, you finally have space to hear it. But that doesn't mean it's easy. Because right after the roar fades…the swirl begins.

I felt it myself.

Coming back into the world—physically stronger, but still fragile in how I saw myself. I had just come through the battle. Now I was supposed to re-engage. I'd scroll through highlight reels on social media. See colleagues at full speed. Watch others bounce back faster than I had. And I'd start comparing. Measuring. Doubting. And the quiet voice got harder to hear.

That's how the swirl works. Not all giants roar. Some disguise themselves as comparison. As envy. As fear of being left behind. Sometimes the swirl is a sideways comment from a coworker. Sometimes it's watching someone else get credit. Sometimes it's the pressure to make up for lost time.

There's a cycle to it: Intention *leads* to disruption. Disruption *triggers* emotion. Emotion *clouds* clarity. You begin with purpose. Then something knocks you sideways. Then the fear rises—shame, frustration, doubt. And suddenly… the voice you need most gets buried. And if you're not grounded, you'll start living in the swirl of everyone else's urgency. It's not just emotional. It's cultural. It's organizational. And if you don't tune in—the swirl becomes your default identity. Loose. Reactive. Unmoored.

David knew this too.

After Goliath, he was brought closer to Saul, Israel's first king and leader at the time. But Saul's welcome wasn't genuine. It was laced with jealousy. The same voice that once celebrated him soon tried to sabotage him. But David didn't retaliate. He didn't get swept into the swirl. He stayed anchored.

Anchored to the voice that called him first. The one that found him in the pasture. The one that whispered purpose when no one else was watching. That kind of clarity isn't loud. It's loyal. It's slow. It's steady. It's grounded. And it's the only way forward after the echo. So pause here for a moment:

- What swirl are you caught in right now?

- What's disrupting your clarity?

- Whose voice are you actually listening to?

You're not late. You're aligning.
You haven't missed your moment.

You're returning to the voice that matters. Because the noise will always be there. The swirl will always try to pull you back. But you also have a choice: To keep chasing volume—or to slow down and tune in to the quiet voice that's been calling you all along. That voice isn't gone. It's just waiting to be trusted again.

FROM HEARING TO HEEDING

It's not just what you hear. It's what you do with it. The quiet voice doesn't change you just because you recognize it. It changes you when you respond. It asks something of you. It doesn't pressure. But it invites you to act.

You can feel purpose stir. You can know, deep down, what truly matters. But transformation begins not in the knowing—but in the doing. That's what I learned in the season after healing. When the whisper of purpose met the practice of movement. It's one thing to hear that you're free. It's another to live like it.

I still remember the first time I rode again. I'd picked up a Catrike MAX—a three-wheeled machine built for stability, strength, and forward motion. I eased into the seat, clipped my feet into the pedals, clicked into gear, and rolled slowly down a gravel path. No one was watching. No stopwatch was running. No medal waited at the end.

Just movement.
Just breath.
Just a quiet voice saying, "This is strength too."

That ride didn't prove anything to anyone. But it restored something in me. I wasn't riding to show I'd bounced back. I was riding because I was becoming someone new. That's what the quiet voice does. It doesn't push you to perform. It invites you to become. And becoming takes practice.

I logged over 600 miles that season. Not out of pressure. But out of joy. Out of presence. Out of the realization that this—the steady return, the faithful repetition—was how a new identity is formed.

And along the way, something else surfaced: Kindness. Not the people-pleasing kind. Not the soft-spoken version fear uses to keep the peace. But the rooted kind. The kind that comes from wholeness. The kind that listens without fixing. Leads without controlling. Sees without judging.

David showed that kind of strength too. He spared Saul—not because he was weak, but because he knew who he was. He wasn't defined by Saul's sabotage. He was anchored in something deeper. That's what kindness looks like when it's powered by purpose, not fear. And for the fear-driven achiever, that shift is everything.

Fear says:

> *Don't rock the boat.*
> *Don't let them down.*
> *Keep proving you're good enough.*
> *When the pressure rises, double down.*

But the quiet voice says:

> **You're free.**
> **You're seen.**
> **You were made to build, not to perform.**
> **Be still and know.**

That's where freedom lives.
In kindness without fear.
In courage without proving.

In small, faithful, intentional action—not to earn identity, but to embody it. Because when you start heeding the quiet voice, everything changes:

- You stop reacting.
- You start becoming.
- You stop rehearsing fear.
- You start responding to freedom.

So let this be the final threshold:
Will you live from the voice of fear—or the voice of freedom?

Will you keep chasing your old name—or respond to the new one being whispered even now?

Because the giant isn't roaring anymore. But the quiet voice still is. And this time, it's calling you. Small steps in freedom are stronger than loud leaps in fear.

Chapter 6

WHEN THE CALLING BURNS: PURPOSE REMAINS

THE ECHOES OF FIRE
When the smoke clears, what still burns underneath?

D.L. Moody (1837-1899), the American evangelist, stood in silence, staring at the ash heap that used to be his city, Chicago. Smoke still rose in thin, curling tendrils. The worst of the flames were gone, but the destruction was complete. Streets that once pulsed with ambition now smoldered in quiet devastation. Somewhere in the distance, a fire still crackled—the final echo of everything that had just burned.

It was October 10, 1871, what later would be known as the Great Chicago Fire. Just hours earlier, fire had raged through Chicago with a fury no one could contain. Moody had been preaching that night—offering words of faith, hope, and love to a packed congregation. As he stood in the ruins the next morning, his voice gone quiet, he couldn't help but wonder: *Did they make it out? Were they safe?* The question burned in him just as fiercely as the fire had burned through the city.

But it wasn't just buildings that were lost. It was everything Moody had built to prove he was enough. The grand Sunday school. The church he had poured his soul into. His platform. The crowded rooms where he had once spoken with passion and purpose—all of it, gone. I remember that feeling in my own way.

The day I received my discharge letter from the Army, I sat with the same kind of silence. It didn't come from a fire — but from the quiet burn of a few printed words: *unqualified, rated, disabled*. The dream of serving went up in smoke. And just like Moody, I felt that ache—the drive to prove I was still strong, still capable, still worthy of the identity I had tied my whole life to.

In the stillness, Moody must have felt it too—the old instinct rising. Rebuild. Push harder. Prove you're stronger than what you've lost. That's what fear says. That's what the giant whispers when everything falls apart.

But then came another voice—quieter, but truer. Pause. Listen. Let what was lost create space for what's meant to be. That moment after the fire feels hauntingly familiar. Because when we stand in the ashes of everything we thought defined us—the image we worked so hard to build—the giant's voice always echoes: "You're not enough." "What if it happens again?" "They'll see you're not who they thought you were."

Those whispers tempt us to rush. To rebuild fast. To perform louder. Anything but pause. Anything but listen. But there's another question waiting in the silence—and it's the one that matters most:

If the work is gone, is there still purpose?

It's a question Moody had to ask. I've asked it too. And if you've ever watched your old identity burn away, you probably have as well.

The fear says:
Without the title, you're nothing.
Without the work, you don't matter.

But what if that's the lie? What if purpose was never about what we built on the outside… but about who we're becoming on the inside?

What if the fire doesn't destroy the truth—but reveals it?

THE ROOTS OF THE FEAR-DRIVEN ACHIEVER

The hustle didn't come out of nowhere. D.L. Moody's instinct to prove himself didn't start in the ashes of Chicago. It started in childhood. When Moody was just four years old, his father died suddenly, leaving his mother alone with nine children and no money. Survival wasn't a metaphor — it was daily life. Every day was a scramble to put food on the table, to keep the family from falling apart.

Moody learned early that he had to contribute — to be more than just another mouth to feed. By seventeen, he'd left home, chasing a better life. But poverty had already planted something deep in him. A script. A pressure. A question. *Will I ever be enough?* He sold shoes by day and chased influence by night, driven by a relentless need to build, to succeed, to matter. The king of the hustle — long before hustle had a name.

When the Chicago fire tore through Moody's life's work, it wasn't just the buildings that burned. It was the fear of losing everything he thought had redeemed his past. Moody likely wondered:

> *Was any of it worth it?*
> *Did I make a difference?*
> *Were the people I preached to still alive?*
> *Did I fail them?*

When you live as a fear-driven achiever, failure isn't just about you. It feels like life or death for someone else. The instinct is to double down — to do more, build faster, push harder — because the stakes feel too high to do anything else. I know that story well.

When I got my discharge letter from the Army, it wasn't just a job ending. It felt like every story I'd ever told myself about identity and worth had just gone up in flames. If I can't serve…Will someone else not make it home? Will a family go without support? Will a village, a unit, a region suffer because I'm not there? It didn't just feel like loss. It felt like guilt. It felt like failure. I had told myself *this* was my calling. This was who I was. And if I couldn't do it anymore, then what was left?

That's the trap of the fear-driven achiever—the belief that if I'm not everything to everyone, then I'm nothing at all. And if I'm nothing, I have no purpose. And if I have no purpose, what's left?

Even now, that echo can still show up in quiet moments — the whisper that says: If you're not building fast… If you're not showing up perfectly…**You're falling behind.** But there's another voice—one that speaks quieter, but truer.

The voice of purpose says: **You're already enough.** You don't have to prove it. Building from fear will never give you peace—and it won't build the legacy you were made for. The fear-driven hustle may have helped you survive once. But it will never help you thrive. What echoes of early survival are still shaping how you lead or live today? Where might the quiet voice of purpose be inviting you to lead differently?

THE QUIET VOICE IN THE ASHES

Sometimes the boldest thing you can do is pause. The temptation to rebuild quickly after loss is real. It's loud. It's strong. And it feels like the only way to prove you're okay. That's the moment fear thrives—in the rush. In the compulsion to post the comeback, curate the next chapter, and show the world (or at least your feed) that you're still standing. But that's not what D.L. Moody did.

Instead of grabbing bricks and rebuilding his church, Moody paused. He stepped away from the ruins of Chicago and traveled to England. Not for escape. Not for rest. But to recalibrate—to find a new rhythm, to let the dust settle, to listen for what really mattered.

In today's terms, it's like going offline when everything in you screams to make a post. It's the difference between reclaiming status and reclaiming identity. We live in a culture that tells us to bounce back like nothing happened. To filter the pain. To package the recovery in perfect lighting and a caption full of inspiration. But real healing doesn't happen in noise. Real change comes when you let the fire burn away what doesn't belong. Fear. Striving. The need to prove. That's what Moody chose. And eventually, so did I.

After my Army discharge, everything in me wanted to dive straight into something new—to prove I was still strong, still capable, still a man. I wanted the next chapter to be louder than the last. To drown out the silence with movement. But somewhere along the way, I found a different rhythm.

My recumbent trike rides became that pause. Not because they fixed everything. But because they made space. Space to breathe. To reflect. To hear the quiet voice beneath the noise. It wasn't escapism. It wasn't distraction. It was an intentional act of listening.

And here's what I learned:

**The fire can only consume what's not real.
What remains—underneath the ash—
is what was already true.**

Like steel in a forge, the heat doesn't destroy. It tempers. It strengthens. And in the stillness, that quiet voice asks a sacred question: What's left when you're no longer trying to prove anything? And the answer… is not emptiness.

It's strength. It's clarity. It's the resilient core of who you truly are—shaped by pressure, refined by heat, free from the fear that once drove you.

This is the tension—and the invitation. To pause. To listen. To let the noise fade long enough to hear the quiet voice of purpose. Because what's left isn't just an echo of who you were. It's the foundation of who you're becoming. Where have you felt the pressure to prove you're still standing–to rebuild fast and loud? What's been revealed in those moments when you paused long enough to let the fear burn away?

REBUILDING FROM PURPOSE, NOT PROVING

When you're no longer trying to impress the world, you can finally impact it. After the Chicago fire, D.L. Moody didn't rush to rebuild his church. He didn't scramble to prove he was still a leader. And he didn't disappear into shame. He paused. He went to England — not for escape, but for silence. For stillness. To hear what came next.

What emerged from that season wasn't a bigger building. It was a bigger mission. One no longer centered on the structures he had lost, but on the people the world often overlooked—the forgotten, the poor, the hungry for hope. That was the pivot. The shift from performing to leading. From fear to purpose. And Moody wasn't alone in that moment of pain.

Around the same time, his close friend and supporter Horatio Spafford experienced unimaginable tragedy when his family was lost at sea. And from that heartbreak came one of the most enduring hymns in history:

> "When *sorrows* like sea billows roll,
> Whatever my lot, Thou hast *taught* me to say —
> **It is well, it is well with my soul**."

Those words weren't denial. They were surrender. They were strength. They were a declaration that purpose doesn't come from pretending the pain isn't real — it comes from leading *through* the pain with quiet trust.

For Moody, those lyrics weren't just comforting. They were convicting. True leadership doesn't come from bouncing back fast. It comes from anchoring in the quiet truth: You're still here. You're still enough. And that's enough to lead with purpose.

King David knew that kind of loss too. He didn't just fight Goliath. He faced sabotage from Saul, betrayal by friends, and years of exile from his own people. The temptation to prove he was still worthy of the crown must have been immense. But in those wilderness years, David learned something deeper. He found a different kind of leadership. Not loud. Not performative. But anchored.

In the Psalms, he wrote: **"Be still, and know…"** David's "be still" wasn't passive. It was powerful. It was an intentional refusal to let fear dictate what came next. That same quiet voice is what Moody heard in the ashes. It's the same voice I eventually heard too.

After my first hip surgery, I was terrified. Terrified of being seen as broken. Terrified of losing my mission, my identity, my place. So I pushed hard. Too hard. I raced back to my Army Reserve role, determined to prove I was still strong. I didn't listen to the pain. I silenced it. I told myself I had to bounce back—fast, clean, complete.

But that push came at a cost.

The suture anchoring my hip tore loose within six months. What was supposed to be recovery became eight years of pain. A worsening limp. A relentless echo of fear whispering: You're failing. You're falling behind. You're succeeding at what doesn't matter.

The second surgery was different. This time, I chose to be still. I chose to listen. I chose to let the quiet voice guide my healing. The recumbent trike rides weren't about performance. They were about presence. About rebuilding from the inside out. This wasn't about reclaiming an identity. It was about creating from one. Not as a survivor scrambling to prove I was okay. But as a leader anchored in purpose — scarred, yes, but whole.

That's what rebuilding from purpose looks like. It's not fast. It's not loud. But it's real. It's the difference between performing to be seen and creating something that lasts. Because when the applause fades…when the metrics stall… when the platform crumbles…the quiet voice still remains. And that voice says: *You're already enough.*

QUIET CONFIDENCE – THE FOUNDATION OF SUSTAINABLE LEADERSHIP

When the noise fades, what kind of leader are you becoming? That's the question D.L. Moody had to face in the ruins of Chicago. He could have rushed to rebuild. He could have fought for recognition, scrambled for control, or collapsed into defeat. But he didn't.

> He chose something different —
> the quiet work of listening.
> Of anchoring.
> Of redefining leadership not by how quickly he bounced back, but by what kind of legacy he would leave behind.

Moody's greatest impact didn't come from the size of what he rebuilt. It came from the depth of what he heard in the silence. "You're still here. You're still enough. And that's enough to build something that lasts." That's quiet confidence. And it doesn't just change you—it multiplies into the people around you. Because quiet confidence isn't about shrinking back or disappearing. It's about knowing exactly who you are—and leading from that place, even when the world expects noise.

King David lived that kind of leadership too. For him, quiet confidence looked like trusting that his identity didn't come from the throne. It wasn't tied to the crown or the approval of the people. It came from being still. From listening to a voice louder than any giant's taunt. David chose to lead from clarity, not chaos. From presence, not performance.

For Moody, it meant choosing mission over monuments. People over platforms. Purpose over proving.

For me, that same quiet confidence came—but only after everything I tried fell apart. After my first surgery failed, I learned a hard truth: Fear-driven momentum always burns out. Fast may look impressive, but it rarely lasts. But the second time—in the healing, in the trike rides, in the silence—something shifted. I discovered that leadership built from the quiet voice wasn't just stronger…

> It was *sustainable*.
> It was *scalable*.
> It was *transformational*
> — not just for me, but for those I led.
> It changed how I defined leadership altogether.

WHEN THE CALLING BURNS: PURPOSE REMAINS

I used to think leadership meant being the strongest voice in the room. The fastest decision-maker. The one who could prove they were still in control. But in the quiet, something new emerged. I became a cultivator. Leadership became less about spotlighting *my* voice—and more about creating space for *others* to find theirs. It became about empowerment. Discernment. Compassion. Not just directing people. But slowing down long enough to see them. To ask better questions. To see the human behind the role.

And when you lead like that, you start to notice things. You see the same hustle and striving in others—the fear disguised as strength, the silent suffering behind the performance. And instead of pushing them harder, you offer something different:

Compassion.
Clarity.
A place to grow.

Because when you lead from quiet confidence, you're not just managing people—you're nurturing them. You're helping them see what's already inside of them. You're drawing it to the surface—like a tree breaking through the soil, rooted in purpose, rising with strength.

That's what rebuilding from purpose looks like. It's not about being seen. It's about seeing others. It's not about proving. It's about cultivating. And in a world obsessed with bounce-backs and bold headlines, quiet confidence isn't weakness it's the foundation of a leader who doesn't just recover… but endures.

For generations.

BUILDING BEYOND THE ECHOES

You're not just leading differently.
You're becoming someone new.

Even after slaying Goliath and leading with courage, David's greatest leadership tests didn't come on the battlefield. They came through heartbreak.

When his own son Absalom rose up to overthrow him, David didn't fight back with noise. He didn't cling to the throne. He didn't scramble to reclaim power. Instead, he led with quiet confidence. The same stillness he wrote about in the Psalms. He knew that leadership rooted in fear crumbles under pressure — but leadership anchored in purpose stands even in betrayal.

David didn't let the echoes of fear or rejection define him. Because his identity wasn't in the crown. It was in being a shepherd. A cultivator. A man after God's heart. He wasn't just building a kingdom—he was becoming someone who could lead one. That's what purpose does. It strips away the noise until what's left is real.

D.L. Moody experienced the same. The fire could have ended everything he built—and for many, it would have. But instead of rebuilding fast, he stayed in England for two years. Two years of listening. Two years of recalibrating. Two years of letting the quiet voice reshape what leadership even meant. When he finally returned to the United States, he didn't rebuild a monument.

He sparked a movement.

Moody turned his focus toward children. Toward working-class families. Toward the people society had overlooked. He didn't lead from the echoes of fear. He led from grounded purpose. And that's why his legacy still echoes today. I've felt those same echoes.

After the Army discharge, fear still whispered: If you're not in uniform, you're not enough. If you're not in service, your life doesn't matter. But in the stillness—in the slow, painful healing—I began to hear something else. That leadership isn't about being unbreakable. It's not about proving anything. It's about making space for others to grow. To listen more than you speak. To cultivate more than you conquer. That's the quiet shift. The moment when calling gives way to purpose.

Because here's the truth:
Calling is what you do.
But **purpose is who you are.**

Put simply: Calling changes – like your job, your title, or your role. But purpose doesn't. It's the steady core of who you are, no matter what season you're in. Purpose endures. It's the steady anchor beneath every storm. The quiet center when fear tries to shout you down. The solid ground that doesn't shake when your title disappears.

The danger is that we confuse the two. We think losing a role means losing our worth. We let fear convince us that if we're not in *this* job or *that* position, we're not fulfilling our purpose. But the quiet voice says otherwise.

You were created to cultivate.
To create. To care.

That's who you are—no matter where you serve. That's what lets you build beyond the echoes, serving as our anchor from the beginning of time (Genesis 1:28).

To lead with clarity and compassion. To see others not as threats to your worth, but as people to be nurtured. To create not for applause, but for impact. To pause. To listen. And to lead from purpose—not from fear.

This is the invitation:

To trade the giant's noise for the quiet voice.
To let go of proving. And build something that lasts.

Because your impact doesn't end with you.
It shapes the future.
And it sets the stage for what's coming next…

A new identity.
A new name.
A new story.
One that begins—when the echoes fade.

Chapter 7

LEADING WHILE LIMPING: REDEFINING STRENGTH IN LEADERSHIP

THE THRESHOLD OF TRANSFORMATION

Picture an ancient, weathered wooden door set deep in the stone of a castle wall. On the other side of that door is the rest of your life. The handle is thick iron—cold to the touch. Even the weight of it in your hand feels like a decision. This isn't a door you wander through by accident. It demands intention. Resolve.

For those of us driven by fear or the need to prove ourselves, this door feels especially heavy. We grip the handle with everything we've been trying to hold together—old identities, striving, the echo of never enough. But sometimes, life brings a moment that becomes the key.

A battle.
A loss.
A pause that shakes something loose.

The door creaks open. And then—choice. To stay in the familiar patterns of fear, or to step forward into the unknown. To let the quiet voice within speak louder than the noise of fear. To push open the door.

Crossing the threshold is never easy. It asks us to release the identity we've built through effort and affirmation. To let go of the scripts that have always worked—until they didn't. It means risking something new. It means leading not to prove, but to become.

And once you step through, there is no going back.

JACOB'S THRESHOLD: WRESTLING IN THE DARK

Jacob's threshold wasn't made of wood and stone. It was a night of wrestling in the dark. Alone with his fears, he wasn't fighting an enemy. He was facing himself—the part that always ran, always grasped, always schemed to stay ahead. He had built his life on performance and fear: deceiving for blessing, striving for position, never resting in who he truly was.

But that night, something shifted.

In the darkness, he refused to let go until he received a blessing. When dawn came, he limped. It wasn't a wound. It was a marker. Jacob had crossed the threshold. He let go of the fear-driven scripts that shaped him. And in the stillness after the struggle, he received a new name: Israel. Not a name earned, but one revealed. Not a title of achievement, but a sign of becoming.

DAVID'S THRESHOLD: FROM ANOINTING TO MERCY

David's crossing didn't start in a battlefield. It started under the stars, alone in a field, still smelling like sheep, stunned by the prophet Samuel's words: **"You'll be king."** He didn't fully understand it yet, but something inside him shifted. Days later, he would stand in a valley facing a giant—not armored like a warrior, but with the quiet courage of a shepherd's heart.

But David's real threshold came later. When Saul hunted him like an enemy. When the caves became his palace. When he held Saul's life in his hands—twice—and spared him. Later, when his own son Absalom rose against him, David could have met rebellion with force. Instead, he offered mercy.

Each time, David gripped the handle of that ancient door. And with every quiet act of restraint, he stepped further away from fear-driven leadership and deeper into strength rooted in stillness. His Psalms bear witness: strength not found in conquest, but in communion.

MOODY'S THRESHOLD: AFTER THE FIRE

That same stillness echoed across centuries in the life of D.L. Moody. The Great Chicago Fire consumed everything he had built—the noise, the ministry, the platform. But when the flames died down, what remained was quiet.

Ashes. Smoldering ruins. And a silence deeper than loss.

In that hush, Moody faced his threshold. He could rebuild from fear, or he could follow a quieter call. He chose faith. He left for England—not just for preaching, but for perspective. And when he returned, it wasn't with noise. It was with purpose. He no longer led to gather crowds. He led to gather souls. Stillness became his new strength.

MY THRESHOLD: THE QUIET CROSSING

I found my own threshold in a cold, dark bedroom. Not in smoke or fire, but in fear. The air was thick—not with loss, but with dread. Giants crouched in the corners of my mind, whispering lies: You'll never be enough. You have to keep proving. Or quit altogether. But in that quiet, I felt it—the handle in my hand. I had a choice. Stay in the shadows of fear. Or step through the threshold into a new way to lead—and live.

That night, I made a vow. To stop proving. To start cultivating. To begin again. I started leading not to be seen, but to see. Not to be known, but to know. And in that stillness, the fear-driven achiever in me fell silent.

I stepped into the new.

Every threshold you cross with quiet courage reshapes not just what you do—but who you are. In the stillness, something new waits for you.

Where in your life do you feel the weight of the handle in your hand? What would it look like to let go of fear-driven scripts—and step into the quiet strength of becoming?

THE POWER OF STILLNESS IN BECOMING

There's a hush that settles after the battle ends. It's the quiet that comes after the noise dies down—the moment after the striving stops, when something deeper has space to rise. It's there, in the stillness, that the old identity begins to fade and the new name starts to take shape. Not in the clamor of performance, but in the clarity that follows surrender.

Stillness is not idleness. It's the soil of transformation. Like the dawn that broke after Jacob's night of wrestling, stillness is where striving ends and the true self emerges limping, maybe, but no longer running. Jacob's new name, Israel, wasn't given in the fight. It came in the hush of morning. After the struggle.

David knew this too. In the silence of the caves. In the stillness of the Psalms. Those hidden places were where his identity as king took root—long before any crown touched his head. His new name wasn't formed in battle, but in the mercy he chose when he could've claimed vengeance. King David—the shepherd king of restraint—grew into that name in the quiet.

D.L. Moody also found his stillness in the ashes. After the fire swept through Chicago, it wasn't the smoke that changed him—it was what came after. In the silence of the morning, stripped of crowds and striving, he heard a new call. His mission wasn't to build platforms. It was to build people.

He said it plainly:
"Our greatest fear should not be of failure, but of succeeding at something that doesn't really matter."

That's the paradox.

Stillness looks like pause. But it holds power. It's not weakness—it's a threshold. The place where fear loses its grip and a new identity begins to form.

The Cycle: Intention → Disruption → Emotion → Fog

For the fear-driven achiever, life is a loop.
- You set out with intention—to lead well, to do good.
- Disruption hits. A conflict. A failure. A loss of control.
- Emotion floods in—fear, shame, anger. The fear of not being enough. The shame of being seen as less. The anger at being overlooked.
- Clarity disappears. You start to doubt yourself, your path, your worth.

So what do you do?
>You double down.
>You grip the old script even tighter.
>You try to outrun the fear by achieving something: Louder. Faster. Bigger.

But in the process, you risk what Moody warned of—succeeding at something that doesn't matter.

STILLNESS: THE SOIL WHERE IT CHANGES

Stillness doesn't just calm your heart. It clears your mind. It breaks the cycle. In the hush, the fog lifts. And in that clarity, something takes root. You begin to lead—not from fear, but from truth.

Like roots growing deep beneath the surface, your new identity forms quietly, unseen at first. But it's real. And it's strong. The old scripts lose their power. And the quiet truth of who you are becoming begins to grow. Stillness is not retreat. It's return.

Return to the voice you've always had—the one that's been whispering your true name beneath all the noise. And in that stillness, something sacred happens:
- You find the courage to create.
- You see the path fear kept hidden.
- You lead with a clarity that performance can't manufacture.

For seasoned leaders, this clarity shapes cultures. It informs decisions. It sharpens strategy. For emerging leaders, these quiet moments unlock innovation. They cut through the clutter of social media and the noise of hustle culture. Stillness is how you hear your own voice again.

THE EVERDAY PRACTICE OF STILLNESS

Stillness isn't reserved for mountaintops or monasteries. It lives in the ordinary.

When I served in the Army Reserve, there was a man in our unit we called "Pops." He joined at the very edge of the top age limit. But what he brought wasn't youth.

It was wisdom.

"Pops" was a brilliant mechanic and a master of mathematics. Every move was calculated. Deliberate. Never reactive. Never fear-driven. Whenever frustration crept in—whether fixing a vehicle or solving a problem—Pops had a ritual. He'd stop. Walk away. Grab a cold Coke. And drink it slowly. By the time he finished, more often than not, the answer had come. Not in the noise—but in the stillness.

For the fear-driven achiever, that kind of pause feels like losing ground. Wasted time. But Pops knew better. Stillness wasn't quitting. It was creating space for clarity to find him. And it did. Every time. There was no panic in his presence. No rush. Just quiet confidence—the kind that comes from leading yourself well before you lead others.

Stillness is not a luxury. It's a foundation. Where might stillness be calling you to pause? Where might a new name, a new clarity, be quietly waiting to take root?

PERSONAL REFLECTION: MY MOMENT OF BECOMING

I didn't become different in one dramatic moment. There was no spotlight. No stage. No sign that said, *"You've arrived."* My becoming unfolded in a quiet place most people have never heard of—a winding gravel path through a rural conservation area called Four Rivers. It started with a problem.

After my second surgery, something shifted again. I felt a mechanical pop. This time, I didn't ignore it. I got it checked. The surgeon confirmed what I suspected—a muscle snapping over bone. No new surgery, but six more weeks of physical therapy. Another summer on hold. Still because of my hip.

I finished therapy feeling better physically, but something inside me whispered: Don't wait for the next setback. Move forward. So I did something unexpected. I bought a three wheeled bicycle, known as a *recumbent trike*—a white Catrike MAX to be exact. Technically, it's what's known as a "tadpole" because of its shape: two wheels in front, one in the back, as you pedal it looks like a tadpole swimming in the water. It cost me $5,000. And a glimmer of hope.

The first ride was brutal. I barely made it around the driveway, relying heavily on the electric assist. But I kept going. Short rides became longer ones. I discovered Four Rivers—a five-mile loop bordered by wetlands, fields, and wildlife. Ducks. Cranes. Turtles. Fish hitting the surface of the water. Most days, I'd see an eagle—sometimes flying directly overhead, like it was trying to figure out what kind of creature I was.

By summer's end, I was riding 20… sometimes 25 miles at a time. Two days a week. Every week. I lost weight. I felt stronger. But more than that—I felt free. Free in a way I hadn't felt in over a decade. But the most important thing that happened wasn't physical. It was subtle. Quiet. Real.

They called the design of my trike a *tadpole* because of the frame. But somewhere along that loop, I realized the name meant something more. Tadpoles don't stay tadpoles. They grow legs—slowly, in still water. And once they leap… they never go back. That was me.

Ride by ride, I was changing. Not just rebuilding strength—but being remade. The physical transformation mirrored something deeper. I was becoming ready to move forward—not just across terrain, but into a new way of life.

Tadpoles don't grow in rivers. They grow in ponds. Still places. Quiet places. That's where their transformation happens. Mine too.

> In the hush of those wetlands, I wasn't just exercising.
> > I was stretching.
> > Praying.
> > Reconciling.
> > Innovating.
> > Becoming.

Stillness wasn't stagnation.
It was incubation.

And once the change took root… there was no going back. I was no longer defined by the hip. I was defining the hip. No longer shaped by fear. I was moving with purpose. The fear-driven achiever inside me—the one who always had to push harder, run faster, prove more—he couldn't survive in that kind of stillness. That's what becoming looked like for me.

Not some epic undoing. But a quiet return. To breath. To strength. To clarity. To a name I'm still learning to live into. Even now—every eagle overhead, every frog croaking from the still waters—they remind me: Stillness makes leaping possible. Stillness isn't where you stop.

It's where you grow legs.

The quiet doesn't mean nothing is happening. It's where strength forms, where new identity is shaped, where fear begins to lose its script. And when the moment comes, you'll realize: the leap was made *possible* by everything that happened in the stillness.

STEPPING INTO THE NEW

There's a place south of where I live—quiet, rural, mostly unknown to those speeding by on the highway. It's called Four Rivers, a conservation area where four separate rivers come together:

- The Osage
- The Marmaton
- The Marais des Cygnes
- The Little Osage

Each river has its own story. Its own terrain. Its own rhythm. Its own origin. But for a moment—right there in that marshland—they run side by side. They don't merge into one. They don't erase each other. They simply share stillness. And then, they continue on—separate but changed. That's what becoming has felt like.

The **Osage** carried my physical story—every painful step, every surgery, every slow return to strength. Its name, drawn from the Osage Nation, speaks of people formed by the middle waters—those who hold ground in in-between places.

The **Marmaton**, rooted in the French word *marmotte* or *marmiton*, whispered what was buried—my emotional undercurrents, the grief I carried silently, the humble service often overlooked. It reminded me of what endured beneath the surface.

The **Marais des Cygnes**, the *marsh of swans*, moved more slowly. It became the spiritual current — the place where mystery lingered, where grace returned. It was there, in that sacred hush, I rediscovered God's nearness. I found stillness again.

And the **Little Osage**, a quieter tributary with the same root name, became the symbol of my emerging identity. It didn't roar. It didn't demand. But it carried the same essence. It was the quiet current of transformation — the part of me that had stopped proving, stopped performing, and started becoming.

At Four Rivers, these stories didn't crash into each other. They were seen together. Not as contradictions, but as convergence. Not erased. Aligned. It reminded me of Jacob. He stood at a river too—alone, in the dark, haunted by fear and unresolved identity. And there, in the wrestling, he was both wounded and renamed. He crossed that river limping— not because he was weak, but because he had been changed. So did I.

My limp wasn't in the same place, but it was real. And I carried it, just like Jacob did—not as a mark of shame, but of remembrance. Because the river doesn't just change your direction. It marks you.

Now, standing in that same stillness, I offer you the quiet invitation: Not to rush forward. Not to blend in. But to notice the rivers that have shaped you.

- What pain or strength has your body carried?

- What emotions have quietly influenced your patterns and reactions?

- What spiritual whispers have lingered across your journey?

- And what part of you—maybe even now— is being renamed?

You don't need to name it all today. But you can **begin**.

Begin to trust that stillness is not absence—
it's awareness.

Begin to believe that you are not fractured—
you are forming.

Begin to live as someone whose name is rising.

Because in the place where your rivers meet, you are not losing yourself. You are stepping into someone full. Someone becoming. Someone who may still walk with a limp… but now walks with a name. And with that name comes something else—something fear could never give you: A sense of calling. Rooted in clarity. A purpose not driven by performance, but anchored in identity.

You're not chasing something out there anymore. You're walking forward from something solid in here.

The limp didn't disqualify you.
The stillness didn't stall you.
They prepared you.

You don't have to figure it all out today. Just start by noticing which river is rising. Let that be enough for now. Because the river moment doesn't just mark you—it sends you. And just like water brings life wherever it flows, you can trust that in the convergence of your story—like at Four Rivers—life will teem again.

For those who lead, that mark becomes more than personal. It shapes how you show up—for your team, your family, your culture. Stillness doesn't just settle your own soul. It sets the tone. It gives others permission to breathe. To lead from clarity is to create clarity. To lead with a limp is to show that strength isn't about hiding your wounds—it's about walking forward with them visible and redeemed.

So maybe now… like Jacob in the early light, or David returning with mercy in his hands, or Moody walking out of the ashes with a quieter fire in his chest…you're ready for the next question:

If I'm no longer who I was… then who am I now?

And that — is exactly where we'll go next.

Chapter 8

WRESTLING, LIMPING, WINNING– REFRAMING THE PAST

THE POWER OF A NAME

There's something sacred about a name.

Not the kind printed on a lanyard or typed into a spreadsheet. But the kind that *calls something out of you*. The kind that doesn't just identify who you are—but reveals who you're becoming.

I once met someone whose name held something beautiful when translated. Her first name meant "Butterfly." Her middle name meant "Meadow." Spoken together, it read like poetry: *Butterfly of the Meadow.*

Each name had meaning on its own—
    Butterfly: transformation, delicacy, motion.
    Meadow: stillness, rootedness, wild beauty.

But together? They told a richer story. A paradox of motion and stillness. Flight and groundedness.

That's the power of a name—it carries layers. Not just labels. Invitations. Revealing that we are not just one thing. We are becoming. She carried that truth in the way she moved through the world. Quiet strength. Observant, gentle—yet resilient. She often hiked in the mountains. And suddenly, her name felt even more accurate—

A butterfly of the mountain meadow.
Drawn to quiet places at altitude.

That's what a true name does. It doesn't just assign—it reveals. It gives us space to wonder: What might be hidden in your name—first, middle, even the ones no one else sees? Because when we begin to *understand* our name—not just what it is, but what it means—we start to see that identity isn't built on pressure or performance.

It's built on something *already spoken.*
Something deep.
Something true.

My name, too, carries layers. Ryan means "little king." Jesse, my middle name, means "God exists" or "God's gift." Put them together—*little king* plus *God exists*—and you get something curious. A quiet kind of sovereignty. Not rooted in ego or entitlement, but in *origin.* A reminder: You come from something bigger. Your identity is connected to *purpose,* not just position.

I was named Jesse after my grandfather. Only later did I realize Jesse was also the name of King David's father—a man remembered not for what he built, but for *who he raised.*

Of course, I didn't understand any of that as a teenager.

One cold October morning, I was volunteering in our church's children's ministry when an usher came in and said, the pastor needed to speak with me. I followed him downstairs, confused. When I opened the sanctuary doors, I was met with silence—every eye turned toward me. The pastor looked at me and said: "You're a Joseph."

He wasn't praising me. He wasn't celebrating something I had done. He was *naming* something *in* me. He said I'd be like Joseph from Genesis—Discerning. Strategic. Able to prepare for what others couldn't yet see. It would cost me, but it would be worth it.

Remember Joseph? Betrayed by his brothers, thrown into a pit and sold into slavery. Joseph suffered thirteen years in Egypt–two of them in prison–before becoming Pharaoh's right hand. Joseph never chose the suffering he endured. But he showed up with faithfulness in every place he landed: in the household of Potiphar, the Egyptian official who owned him as a slave; in the silence of a prison cell, where he was still a prisoner, yet entrusted with the care of the other prisoners; and eventually in the halls of Pharaoh's palace, preparing an entire nation for a great famine still years away. Joseph wasn't driven by ambition. He was led by wisdom. He didn't rise because he sought influence, but because he obeyed the quiet inner voice of truth–and that obedience saved a nation, and the very brothers who once left him for dead.

That naming moment planted something deep inside me. Like a seed. A word that knew where it was going—before *I* did.

Looking back, I realize now: that name 'Joseph' wasn't about *arrival*. It was about *identity*—one that would be formed in the shadows, not the spotlight. Because that's how names work. Joseph didn't walk in his calling until after the prison. David wasn't king the day he was anointed. Jacob didn't receive his new name without a limp.

And me? I didn't leave that church service with a promotion. I left with a new lens. A name I didn't fully understand. But I carried it. And over time, I started to walk in it. Not all at once. Not by force. But by unfolding. By becoming. Even in my own kind of prison—the one shaped by pain, doctors' appointments, and a hip that wouldn't heal—I still kept that name.

Sometimes a name is spoken before you're ready. But it's still yours. And if no one has ever spoken a name over you, you can still discover one. The truest names aren't invented. They're revealed. And as we'll see next—some names we carry by choice. Others were handed to us… without asking.

THE NAME YOU DIDN'T CHOOSE

We don't always get to choose the names we carry. Some are handed to us before we even know who we are. Not the kind written on a birth certificate—but the kind whispered, repeated, implied. Labels that follow us like hashtags. Shaping our reputations, our expectations, our inner narratives.

They come from family dynamics, cultural pressures, performance metrics, or wounds we didn't ask for.
The anxious one.
The smart one.
The black sheep.
The golden child.
The screw-up.
The reliable one.

The fixer.
The one who always ruins it.
The strong one.
The soft one.
The sidekick.
The quiet one.
The third-wheel.
The star.

These are names. They may not be official, but they act like them. And names come with scripts. And scripts shape stories. Some of those stories are lies—giant-sized lies. Repeated often enough, believed deeply enough, that we mistake them for truth. We obey them like actors in someone else's play.

Let's revisit the people we've walked with so far:

Jacob was literally named "Deceiver." Supplanter. Manipulator. Trickster. In modern terms, he might be called: The one who always has an angle. The guy you can't quite trust. The hustler who's afraid he's not enough. Maybe Jacob believed the lie that he had to fight for everything—or be forgotten. That no one would bless him unless he stole it first.

David, despite being anointed king, was dismissed. First as the kid watching sheep. Then as the problem child of Saul's jealousy. Later as the washed-up father of a rebellious son. What were his labels? Too young. Too emotional. Too risky. Peaked early. Messed up. Not king material. Even Goliath, the first enemy David ever faced, mocked him: "Am I a dog, that you come at me with sticks?" Translation: You're a joke. You don't belong here. The giant's lie? David doesn't matter. He's not enough. He's not ready.

Joseph was called "Dreamer"—but not as a compliment. He was mocked for thinking too big. When his brothers threw him in a pit, they weren't just attacking his body—they were trying to bury his identity. His modern label? Too much. The weird visionary. The guy who talks big but hasn't done anything yet. The lie? Your dreams are delusions. Hope is dangerous. Shrink.

Moody, before the fire, was successful—loud, scrappy, platform-famous. He was "winning" by every visible metric. But inside, he was fragmented. Gifted, yes. But still driven. Still striving. Still missing the deeper alignment that roots impact in identity. In today's language, we might say: He was crushing it. But he didn't know why he was running. The lie? Public impact is the same as inner transformation. That motion equals meaning.

And me? I've carried some of those names, too. Fear-driven achiever. People-pleaser. Quiet one. Always-on fixer. Gifted—but quietly afraid I'd burn out before it ever counted. I spent years trying to outrun the names I never agreed to. Thinking maybe if I succeeded enough, they'd start calling me something else. But here's what I've learned: There's a cycle.

- When you don't know who you are…
- You try to prove what you're worth.
- That need to prove leads to performance.
- Performance leads to exhaustion.
- Exhaustion leads to collapse… or reinvention.
- But if that reinvention is still driven by fear, the whole cycle resets—just with a new name.

Endless loop. New costume. Same ache.

And sometimes the name you didn't choose… is "Leader." Not everyone wears that title because they chased it. Some of us were handed it—because we were competent. Consistent. Good under pressure. We could deliver. We could be trusted. We could hold things together when others fell apart. For a while, it felt like a badge of honor. But if your identity isn't rooted, even the word "Leader" can become a cage.

- If you were promoted for being the one who always figures it out…what happens the first time you can't?
- If your worth has been tied to your output… how do you rest without guilt?
- If your team, your family, your church, or your organization looks to you for answers… who are you when you don't have any?

The fear-driven achiever often enters leadership to applause—but underneath the platform is a whisper: Keep going or they'll see the cracks. Double down. You cannot fail.

Leadership, when disconnected from identity, only amplifies the cycle:
- You perform → so they promote.
- You achieve → so they expect more.
- You deliver → but at what cost?

And one day, you're left wondering:
Am I leading from wholeness—or just from momentum?

Sometimes the most dangerous names are the ones everyone praises—because they mask the ache underneath.

"Leader" isn't a bad name.
But it's not your only one.
And it should never be your first.

You remember the quote we started this book with? "Our greatest fear should not be of failure, but of succeeding at something that doesn't really matter."
D.L. Moody

The fear-driven achiever often *succeeds*—but can't *rest*. Not because they haven't done enough—but because they don't know who they are *without* the doing. Stillness, as we saw in the last chapter, isn't passive. It's *active*. It's where clarity returns. Where old names begin to fall away. It's where the question rises:

What if I'm not who they said I was?
What if I'm not even who *I* thought I was?
What if the name I didn't choose... isn't mine anymore?

And yet, even when we begin to see the old name no longer fits, we still wrestle with it. It clings to us in quiet moments. Resurfaces in our reactions, our fears, our inner monologue. Identity doesn't change by willpower alone. It's wrestled out—like Jacob in the dark, grappling with his past, desperate for a new name, terrified of what might come with it. Everything on the line. Because the fear-driven achiever doesn't just *walk away* from the old name—they have to confront it.

What label have you performed your way into?
You are *not* what they called you.

WRESTLING WITH THE OLD NAME

There's a difference between who you are and what you do. But for many of us, those lines get blurry. Especially when we're good at something. Especially when that something meets a need, earns applause, or helps people.

A calling can become a crown.
A job can become a name.
A name can become an identity.

And once people start calling you by that name, it's hard not to believe that's who you *are*. That's why losing a title, switching careers, burning out, or stepping back can feel like grief. Because it's not just the work that ends—it's the identity we tied to it. But sometimes, the loss isn't a dead end. It's the *wrestling before the blessing*.

Jacob, in the dark. "And Jacob was left alone. And a man wrestled with him until the breaking of day." Genesis 32:24. The night before Jacob crossed the river to face Esau— his brother, his past, his guilt—he found himself utterly alone. Not just physically, but emotionally. Alone with the weight of everything he had done, and everything he feared was coming.

All his life, Jacob had lived *up* to his name. Heel-grabber. Deceiver. Manipulator. Always reaching. Always scheming. Always afraid of being overlooked, outmatched, left behind. His name told the story of his struggle. And his struggle had shaped how he survived. Now, at the edge of a new beginning, he found himself in a fight he couldn't control.

WHEN YOU BORROW A NAME TO BE BLESSED

Before the wrestling match in the dark, there was another defining moment in Jacob's life— the day he pretended to be someone else to receive a blessing. He dressed up like Esau. His older brother. The favored one. Just to hear their father speak the words he'd always longed for.

"Who are you, my son?" "I am Esau," Jacob replied. And in that moment, something fractured. Not just in Jacob—but in Esau too. Jacob learned to *perform* for love. Esau lost more than his birthright—he lost trust, voice, identity.

When identity is built on deception, on becoming what others want just to be seen or chosen, it never satisfies. It blesses the *mask*, not the man. That line isn't just ancient. It's now. Social media has made it easier than ever to curate our identities, to perform for validation, to hide behind what gets the most likes. We show the good. We hide the bad. We chase view counts. We choose relevance over rest. Jacob walked away with the inheritance—but not with peace. He carried the weight of pretending, the shame of wondering if he was lovable *without* the costume. So he ran.

WHEN IDENTITY CLINGS TOO TIGHTLY TO CALLING

For the fear-driven achiever, the line between doing and being is nearly invisible.

- The teacher becomes the one who holds everything together.
- The entrepreneur becomes the visionary who can't afford to fail.
- The pastor becomes the spiritual rock others lean on.
- The parent becomes the only stable force in the family.

Eventually, it's not just what you do—it's who you believe you are. But what happens when that title is stripped away? When the business folds? When the church shrinks? When the team no longer follows? When the kids grow up?

If your identity was fused to your role, then losing the role *feels like losing yourself.* That's what Jacob was facing.

Jacob had built a life through striving. He had wealth. Family. Position. But no peace. Not with himself. Not with God. So when the mysterious figure wrestled him in the night, God wasn't just grappling with Jacob's *body*. He was grappling with his *name*. The struggle Jacob had spent his life avoiding—finally caught up with him. "Who are you?" Not, "What have you built?" Not, "What have you achieved?" But… "What's your *name*?"

"Jacob," he replied. And that moment—naming it—was the beginning of releasing it. Then came the reply: "Your name will no longer be Jacob, but *Israel.*" God wasn't just changing Jacob's *story*. He was changing Jacob's *identity*. He was severing the man from the mask—separating the *calling* from the *false identity* it had been wrapped in.

THE OLD NAME WAS NEVER WASTED

What they called you, what you called yourself, the names born from pain, hustle, shadow, or survival—they weren't wasted.

They were like rivers.
Currents that shaped your path.

Jacob's name told a story of struggle. Of reaching, grasping, contending. That striving came with a cost—but it also formed resilience, insight, hunger. When God renamed him *Israel*—"the one who wrestles with God"—He didn't erase Jacob. He *redeemed* him. He honored the journey by transforming it.

Like the four rivers that meet at Four Rivers Conservation Area—your past identities may have flowed from different sources: Pain. Ambition. Survival. Faith. But now they converge—flowing forward under a *new heading*.

You're not asked to throw the old name away. You're asked to *carry it differently*. Through the lens of grace. Of truth. Of purpose. In my own life, there are seasons I used to resent—jobs I discounted, assignments I tried to forget. But now? I treasure them. Not because they were easy. Not because I enjoyed them. But because they formed the ground I now stand on. The struggle wasn't just *on* the path to blessing. It was part of the *composition* of it.

THE COST OF THE NEW NAME

Jacob didn't walk away the same. He limped. That wasn't punishment. It was a *marker*. A sacred reminder. He had been changed in a way performance could never undo. Permanently. The limp was evidence of the struggle—but also evidence of the *blessing*.

> And that's what identity work feels like:
> A wrestling in the dark.
> A surrender of what was familiar.
> A confrontation with the false self.
> A limp that proves something sacred happened.

To the leader—the limp you carry isn't your disqualification. It's what makes you trustworthy. You've been broken in a way that makes others feel safe bringing their *whole* selves to the table. And your team will be better for it.

Calling is not the core. Purpose is. You may be a leader, a parent, a builder, a fixer, a preacher, a protector—but *those* are assignments. Not your name. Your purpose runs deeper. It's the rooted truth of *who you are becoming*. It is *why* you were created—not just *what* you do. And it's not threatened by job loss, title change, or failure. You were *you* before they gave you the title. And you'll still be *you* when it's gone. That's the gift of wrestling.

You may walk with a limp—but you no longer walk with a lie. And there is freedom in that. You are not the name they gave you. You are not even the name you gave yourself. You are the name that comes after the wrestling.

RECEIVING THE NEW NAME

The new name doesn't crash in with fireworks. It doesn't shout or arrive on a stage. It *whispers*. It doesn't wait for when you feel ready. It comes when you're *willing*. You don't earn it through effort. You *walk into it*—usually limping.

There's no instruction manual. No thunder from the clouds. No booming voice. But I remember when it began to make sense. It was just before my second surgery. My limp was at its worst. The pain, constant. The frustration, compounding. The sense of hopelessness, overwhelming.

I was weary.
Physically broken.
Mentally strained.
Emotionally thin.

And in that very season—unexpectedly, divinely—I was placed at the children's hospital, overseeing critical supply chains just as the first wave of the coronavirus pandemic hit. Leaders I admired—people I respected—many of them faltered. Some froze. Others folded. Like a giant had just called them out.

But I didn't rise by strength. I moved forward with a limp. And yet… with *clarity*. I knew what needed to be done. I knew when to push, when to pause, when to act. It wasn't ego. It wasn't spotlight. It was quiet strategy. Provision. A deep knowing—that *this* was what I'd been prepared for all along. Even if I hadn't seen it coming.

There was peace. Not the kind that comes after resolution— but the kind that shows up *in the storm*. While others scrambled, I didn't panic. I didn't freeze. I was still limping. But I was clear. There was a calm in my chest and a clarity in my mind that didn't feel like mine. It felt like a gift. A signal. A whisper: You're walking in your name now.

Not because I had earned it. Not because I had arrived. But because the striving had *ceased*. I wasn't performing. I wasn't posturing. I was *present*. Moving with wisdom, instinct, and peace—the kind that only comes from one place. That peace didn't mean I had it all figured out. (I didn't.) It meant I had nothing to *prove*. And that's when I knew— this wasn't about doing more. It was about becoming someone *different*.

Joseph never asked to be Pharaoh's right hand. He didn't chase the platform. But after the pit, after the silence, after the prison—he stepped into his name. Not just Joseph, the favored son. But Joseph, the *preserver of life*. Not just for Egypt. But for his own people. His own family—who would have starved without the very role he was prepared for through suffering.

>Joseph's wisdom didn't come from the palace.
>It was forged in the shadows.
>Falsely accused.
>Forgotten.
>Refined in the dark.

So when Pharaoh placed the signet ring on his hand, it wasn't a promotion. It was a *recognition* — of who he had already become.

>Your name might come the same way.
>Spoken not in triumph, but in trial.
>Not in applause, but in silence.

You'll be called "Leader" and want to reject it. You'll be called "Healer," "Builder," "Joseph" and feel the weight of it before the fit. But over time, you realize: You're not being asked to wear a costume. You're being asked to walk in *truth*. And there is freedom in that truth.

Even if you're not sure you're ready, the *calm* you carry becomes a signal. Not of perfection—but of *alignment*. Especially for leaders—peace isn't weakness. It's clarity under pressure. It's your quiet edge. And it's contagious. It settles your team. It steadies the storm.

Remember what Moody said:
"Our greatest fear should not be of failure, but of succeeding at something that doesn't really matter."

This is why the name *matters*.
It roots you when success whispers lies.

It centers you when performance tries to reclaim the throne. It pulls you back to your *why*—and to *whom* you're doing it for.

Where have you experienced peace in the middle of pressure?

Could that moment have been a signal—not of your strength, but of your identity?

You don't have to strive to earn your name.
You only have to walk in the peace that proves it's already yours.

Remember:
You are not the name fear gave you.
You are the one who walked through it.

Peace isn't passive.
It's how strategic clarity survives pressure.

Chapter 9

WALKING INTO PURPOSE: LIVING WITH A NEW IDENTITY

THE LIMP IS A SIGNAL

You don't walk the same after you've been renamed.

Something shifts in your stride. Maybe it's slower now. Maybe it's less explosive. But it's more anchored—more aware. For Jacob, it was literal. After wrestling through the night and receiving a blessing from God, he walked away with a limp. A permanent mark carved into his body that testified: something sacred happened here. There was no going back. He had crossed a threshold. He wasn't who he used to be.

Your limp might not be as visible. Maybe it's a scar. A diagnosis. The hesitation in your voice before you speak. The job you had to leave. The relationship you don't talk about. The part of your story you've been managing in silence. But you still carry the memory of what it took to become who you are. And here's the truth: **The limp is not your weakness. It's your witness.** I know this because I live it.

I walk differently now—literally. Two surgeries later, seven scars across my hip, and a deeper one no MRI could see. Years of limping redefined what I thought strength was supposed to look like. It wasn't about getting back to who I used to be. It was about becoming someone new—more grounded, more honest, more me.

You may still feel like your limp is something to hide. You may try to explain it away, minimize it, push through it, normalize it. But your limp is the proof you survived. It's a mark of faithfulness. An external echo of an internal becoming. And it's not just Jacob. It's not just me.

Every leader who walks in a name that wasn't forged by fear—but revealed through fire—carries something changed. The limp doesn't make you less worthy of the road ahead. It proves you're ready to walk it differently. If you choose to.

You don't have to keep up with everyone else. You don't have to impress. You don't have to go viral on TikTok. You just have to keep walking. And let the limp say what words no longer need to.

Maybe you haven't had your big "limp moment" yet. But you've felt the crack. The pressure to pretend. The ache of holding it all together. Don't wait for a collapse to become real. You can walk in your name now—before the breaking. So let me ask you:

- What parts of your story carry a limp?
- Are there scars people can see?
- Or are they quiet, internal weights?
- How might those wounds be shaping who you're becoming?

Even if you haven't reached the breaking point, where do you feel the pressure to pretend? What would it look like to walk forward—real, imperfect, honest? However you've walked so far—limping, sprinting, or stumbling—what matters most now is that you keep walking. Because this is your name.

THE SCARS ARE STORIES

You can hide a limp for a while. But scars? Scars stay. Some fade. Some don't. Some stay hidden under clothing or polite conversation. Others we trace with our fingers when no one's watching.

I have seven scars from two hip surgeries. Small, quiet lines that weren't there before. They mark the pain I walked through—but they also mark the path I walked out. For a long time, I saw them as damage. Evidence of failure.
Proof I wasn't strong enough. But that's not what scars are. Not anymore.

Scars, by definition, mean the bleeding has stopped. They don't just tell the story of the wound—they tell the story of the healing. Of survival. Of resilience. Of a body that didn't give up. Each of my seven scars carries the echo of a different giant I had to face: Fear. Control. Collapse. Silence.
Each one left something behind. But now, they speak of who I've become.

If you're a fear-driven achiever, this is hard to accept. You're used to moving fast. To pushing through. To proving you're fine before anyone sees you sweat. When things fall apart, you double down. You execute with perfection.

Scars? They feel like reminders of when you weren't strong enough. When you didn't see it coming. When you lost control. Instead of honoring the healing, you try to outrun the evidence. But the thing you're most afraid of showing—the moment you cracked—might be the very thing that makes your leadership trustworthy. I've learned that firsthand.

Early in my leadership journey, I didn't ask for help. I didn't want to seem weak. I doubled down. I powered through. But eventually, I realized: **Silence isn't strength. It's isolation.** The more I've learned to name the places I've limped through, the more connection I've built—with my team, and with others.

Now when I say, "I see you. I've been there. Don't do what I did," I'm not leading from theory. I'm offering my scars. Not as a flex. But as an invitation. Because I want others to start higher than I did. To build on what cost me something—so they can go further than I've gone.

Here's the truth: You don't have to be in charge to carry scars. Scars aren't just for leaders. They're for anyone who's walked through something and is still standing. They're milestones. They're markers. They're evidence that you've lived. So maybe the real question isn't: Do you have scars? Maybe it's:

- What story are they telling now?
- What scars—physical or otherwise—have you been hiding or minimizing?
- What would change if you let them speak, not of what broke you, but of what healed you?
- Can you name one of your giants—not to glorify the pain, but to give your healing a voice?

THE LIMP YOU'VE LEARNED TO LIVE WITH

You can get so used to limping that you forget you're doing it. You start building your life around it—adjusting your schedule, your posture, your pace. You carry the pain like it's normal. Until someone asks, "Are you okay?" And you realize: you've just been managing it, not healing from it.

I know that rhythm too well.

For years, I adapted. I worked around the pain—physically, emotionally, mentally, even spiritually. The first surgery didn't solve everything. The second helped, but there were still moments where every step carried a twinge. And in leadership, I mirrored the same pattern. I limped quietly. I didn't talk about it. I got really good at succeeding with a limp. Which sounds noble—until you realize that strength rooted in suppression eventually collapses.

After nearly a decade—from the first failed surgery to the second—I can tell you this:

It's not worth it.

There's a difference between walking with a limp and hiding one. One is honest. The other is driven by fear. And fear always whispers the same lies:

Push through.
Don't show weakness.
Don't slow down.

It trains you to survive, but never to heal.

At the height of my physical pain—just before the second surgery—my life was on autopilot: Wake. Limp. Work. Limp. Sleep. Repeat. It wasn't just my body that was hurting. It was the way I led. The way I tried to prove I was still strong. And that pattern showed up everywhere. Fear had quietly built a culture—inside me, around me. It shaped how I made decisions. How I communicated. How I saw myself. I had become a master at compensating for the limp—but never confronting the giant behind it.

That's what fear does. It doesn't just hurt you. It shapes you. And if left unchallenged, it names you. But the good news? Everything changed when I stopped running and started telling the truth. Not just about the pain—but about the posture I had been holding for far too long. That's what Jacob had to confront too.

After a life of deceiving and striving, he found himself alone by a river, on the eve of facing Esau—the brother he betrayed. He wrestled through the night. Not just with an angel, but with his identity. And by morning, he walked away limping—but also renamed. No longer Jacob, the striver. Now Israel, the one who struggled and survived.

He didn't get a painless blessing. He got a sacred wound. And maybe that's what some of us carry, too. We think the limp is punishment. But it's actually transformation. For fear-driven achievers, this is especially hard to admit.

You've built your identity on how much you can carry. You've taken pride in pushing through without complaint. You've worn pain like a badge. You've confused endurance with purpose. But that doesn't make it healed. It just makes it hidden. And what you hide, you can't redeem.

Redemption doesn't erase the past. It reassigns it. It's the shift from: "This is the thing that *hurt* me" to "This is the thing that *shaped* me." When pain is hidden, it festers. But when it's named, it can be reframed—into wisdom, into clarity, into compassion. That's what redemption does. It takes what fear tried to use against you, and turns it into what purpose can build upon.

Some of us have learned to spiritualize our limp. We professionalize it. We turn it into a personality: "That's just how I lead." "That's just how I cope." "That's just who I am." But deep down, we know that's not our real name. It's the echo of the old one. It's the voice of the giant still whispering in our ear. Still trying to define us by pain, not purpose.

But hear this:
The limp doesn't disqualify you. It identifies you.

Not as broken, but as blessed. As someone who's wrestled with the old—and is walking into the new. Into a future filled with hope and purpose.

The key is telling the truth about the limp. You don't need to announce it to the world. You don't need to put it on a T-shirt or tattoo it on your body. But you do need to stop pretending it isn't there. Because the longer you pretend, the harder it is to walk in your true name. And the more ground fear will steal from you. But when you stop hiding? Something shifts.

Your limp becomes a lighthouse. A signal to others that healing is possible. Not in spite of pain—but through it. Like the four rivers, your story flows from many sources: Old wounds. Past decisions. Regrets. Names you were called. But those rivers don't muddy the water. They make it deep.

So walk with your limp. Let it remind you that you've been changed. But don't let it keep you from moving forward. You are more than what hurt you. Your limp doesn't define your worth. It reveals your story. And your story still has room to move.

THE SCAR AND THE NAME

Some scars are public. Others are hidden. But all of them speak. They're the aftermath of the fight—the visible mark that something happened, and that somehow, you made it through. Scars aren't shame. They're evidence. Not just that you were hurt, but that healing is already underway.

Jacob walked away from his divine wrestling match with a limp. But the miracle wasn't just that he limped. It's that he walked away at all. That limp was his scar—permanent, undeniable. And he didn't hide it. He didn't cover it with robes. He didn't make excuses. He didn't overcompensate to prove he was still strong. He just kept walking. Yes, limping. But leading—with the mark of transformation visible to everyone who saw him, for the rest of his days.

And he didn't just walk. He became a patriarch. The man once called "Deceiver" became the father of twelve sons. Those sons became the twelve tribes of Israel. A nation was born from the man who refused to hide his wound.

> His scar didn't set him back.
> It launched him forward.
> And it's not just biblical.
>
> It's personal.

I carry seven scars from my hip surgeries. They're carved into my skin, yes—but also into memory. For a long time, I tried to conceal them. They felt like failure etched in flesh. But now I see them differently. Each one is a line drawn across the border of who I used to be. Not signs of what I lost— but proof of what I lived through. And of who I'm still becoming.

Scars don't mean you went back to normal. They mean you crossed over. They're thresholds. Lines burned by blade or fire or time—separating the before from the after. They mark the place where pain ended and becoming began. And that matters—because sometimes the scar isn't from what was done to your body. Sometimes the deepest scars come from what was said.

Goliath never touched David. He didn't have to. He shouted. He labeled. He tried to define David with fear— before the first stone ever flew. That tactic hasn't changed.

Today, our giants use ridicule, hashtags, callouts, and shame. Sometimes the most painful scars come from what was posted, assumed, or left unsaid. But David didn't let fear name him. And neither should you.

Your legacy isn't defined by what was shouted at you— but by the truth you choose to walk in. That choice is not passive. If you stay silent, you silently agree with the giant. But you can choose otherwise. You can stand. You can say, *"No. You move."* So let me ask you: What scars—seen or unseen— have shaped who you're becoming? Have you been trying to hide them? Or are you ready to let them speak? Because your limp doesn't limit your worth. It carries your story.

There's still ground ahead—and it's yours to walk.

THE LEGACY OF THE LIMP

Not every legacy is built on strength. Some are built on survival. Not the glossy, highlight-reel kind of survival. Not the comeback story wrapped in fanfare and hashtags. But the kind that limps across the finish line—scarred but still standing. That's the kind of legacy that tells the truth. The kind that invites others to keep going.

Jacob limped into legacy with a new name. No longer the deceiver. Now a father. The patriarch of twelve sons—who would become the foundation of a nation. His pain reshaped his posture. His limp redefined his leadership.

David fled into caves before he ever sat on a throne. But when his time came, he passed on more than just a crown. He passed on blueprints for a temple he never got to build. He left a legacy of mercy, music, and God-breathed imagination.

Joseph bore the weight of betrayal and prison long before he held a signet ring. But it was the wisdom born in those shadows that saved a people from famine. He redefined what it means to lead with both strategy and compassion.

D.L. Moody, a 19th-century preacher who helped shape modern evangelism, came back from the ashes of Chicago with fewer words but deeper fire. The man who once shouted found his strength in stillness. His second act reached farther than his first because it was rooted differently—anchored in purpose, not performance. He didn't lose his leadership—he deepened it. Presence, not projection, became the gift he gave others.

And I've limped forward, too.
Through surgeries.
Through setbacks.

What felt like a prison sentence—like Joseph. Through long nights, whispered prayers, cold bedrooms, and the exhaustion of proving. But still—I showed up.

I showed up at a children's hospital in the middle of a global pandemic, right when my limp was at its worst. While others I respected buckled under the weight of uncertainty, I found myself strangely calm. Not strong—surrendered. Not loud—clear. In that moment, I knew I was walking in my new name. No fear. No panic. No proving. Just peace.

And across the past decade, I've had the humbling honor of serving thousands of children, families, and caregivers. Not just with logistics. With presence. With steadiness. With peace. Not perfectly. But faithfully. That, too, is legacy. And it's why I share my limp with you. Not to impress. To invite. Not to compare. To call.

Because the same quiet strength that steadied me in the storm? It can steady you too. You don't need a platform. You don't need a perfect past. You just need to decide—your pain will not be wasted.

Let your limp tell the truth.
Let your scars point the way.
Let your story give someone else the courage to stand.

That's the echo of legacy.
It's what endures.

YOUR GIANTS ARE LYING TO YOU

We still speak their names:
Jacob. Joseph. David. Moody.
What connects them isn't perfection. **It's pattern.**

Each faced breaking.
Each walked through shadows.
Each emerged quieter—but truer.

They chose faith over fear. They were given a new name. And with it, a new way of being—of leading—of lasting. None of them knew, in the moment, that they were building a legacy that would outlive them.

They were just faithful—with the limp, with the prison, with the cave, with the ashes. And their lives remain.

Not as monuments.
But as mirrors.

They show us what's possible when pain is no longer wasted. When names are reclaimed. When fear loses its grip. When leadership becomes surrender, not performance.

And that same thread?

It runs through you, too.

Chapter 10

THE RIPPLE EFFECT – WHEN YOU MULTIPLY THE SHIFT

THE ECHO RETURNS: 25 YEARS LATER

I hadn't thought about that night in years.
But the memory didn't knock—it hummed.
It rose in the quiet like something waiting to be noticed.

It was the high school cafeteria. Not during lunch, but after hours. The long tables had been folded and rolled to the side. The tile floor swept bare, just enough space cleared for someone to call it a dance. Colored lights spun lazily from a borrowed DJ booth. The music hovered awkwardly in the air—too loud for real conversation, not loud enough to drown out the noise inside.

I was near the far wall, somewhere between the vending machines and the exit, pretending not to exist.

And then she walked across the room.

But really, she'd crossed it long before that night. She was the one who asked my parents if I could go to the dance. Directly. Boldly. Not as a favor, not on a dare. She wanted me there—and I knew it. Even then, I knew it.

She saw me in a way I hadn't yet learned to see myself. Quiet strength. Kindness without pretense. She was sunlight in motion. She walked across that cafeteria with a confidence that didn't need attention. And she offered me her hand. She asked me to dance. And I froze.

Not because I didn't want to go—absolutely, I wanted to—but fear got there first. And instead of reaching back, I shut down. I stayed planted. I told myself it didn't matter. That maybe she was just being nice. That she probably treated every guy like that. I buried the moment in dismissiveness—like I had done with so many others.

But the truth?
I liked her.
She liked me.
And we both knew it.
I just didn't know how to be me yet.

Years later, I realized what that moment had really been—not a chance to dance, but an invitation to be known.

And I missed it.

Not because I was cruel or indifferent or too slow—but because I was afraid. Afraid to break the image I had been curating: the quiet one, the composed one, the achiever, the smart one. Dancing with her would have meant stepping outside of that self-made role. It would have meant being seen. It would have meant being free.

THE RIPPLE EFFECT – WHEN YOU MULTIPLY THE SHIFT

I realize now what I couldn't then: the *little king* had been invited to dance with the *butterfly of the mountain meadow*—and he said no. Not because he didn't care, but because he didn't know he was allowed to be that boy.

The echo came back to me—not in a dream, not in a flashback—but in the stillness of reflection. And this time, I didn't shame the boy I once was. I didn't turn away. I saw him—standing near the exit, frozen behind his own stillness. I saw him clearly. Not as a failure, but as someone becoming.

The moment hadn't changed. I had. Because sometimes healing doesn't mean rewriting the past. It means telling the truth about it. It means finally saying what that boy couldn't: **I wanted to dance with you.** And somehow—even that truth, spoken too late—still creates a ripple.

The lights had been off in the cafeteria that night, except for the DJ's rotating beam casting slivers of red and blue across the floor like a slow-moving kaleidoscope. Everything else was shadow. A strange glow—a little too dim to see clearly, a little too exposed to feel hidden.

I think about that darkness now.

How easy it is to judge the past with the clarity of present light. How tempting it is to shame the boy who froze, as if he should have known better. But here's the truth: We can only walk in the light we've been given.

Back then, my world was dim—fear-driven, performance-based. I didn't yet know how to name what I was feeling, much less act on it. And if I stumbled, it wasn't because I was careless—it was because I couldn't see.

The dance wasn't a failure. It was a moment of formation. A boy learning what it meant to be invited—and realizing, years later, what it means to say yes.

Light expands. Awareness grows. And with it comes accountability—not in shame, but in stewardship. The ripple begins when we stop blaming the darkness and start multiplying the light.

Maybe your story doesn't include a cafeteria. Maybe it wasn't a girl, a song, and a hand you didn't take. But I wonder… was there a moment you didn't reach for? A truth you swallowed to keep the image intact? A whisper that said *move*, but fear kept your feet glued in place?

We all have echoes. Moments we buried or explained away. Opportunities we missed—not because we were weak, but because we didn't yet know we were allowed to say yes. To want. To be seen. To be known. The details will differ. But the ache is familiar. And the good news?

Clarity comes. Light grows. And even the echoes we once feared can become part of someone else's healing—if we're willing to stop hiding them. That's where legacy begins.

LEGACY BEGINS NOW, NOT SOMEDAY

Light doesn't just change what you see. It changes what others see *through* you. That's the quiet truth about legacy. It rarely announces itself. It rarely feels like it's happening in real time. But every time you respond to the light you've been given—when you tell the truth, risk vulnerability, extend grace, or break silence—you're multiplying something.

And people notice. Sometimes it's subtle—a shift in your tone, a new steadiness in your presence, a question you're finally willing to ask or no longer afraid to answer. Other times, it's seismic. A choice you make that rewrites a generational pattern. A boundary you hold that someone else watches and learns from. A story you finally share that gives someone else language for their own.

That's the ripple.

It's not just about influence. It's about *integrity*—and it begins the moment you stop waiting to arrive and start living from who you truly are.

The real you.
Not the version fear helped you create.
Not the mask worn by the fear-driven achiever.

You don't have to have it all figured out to begin.
You don't need a platform to carry light.
You don't need a title to start a legacy.
You just need to be faithful with the light
you've been given.

For those in leadership—formal or informal—the implications run deep. Because when you carry light, people orient themselves around you. They look for signals. They watch what you do in the moments you think no one sees. And whether you intend to or not, you're multiplying something.

The only question is… what?

Are you multiplying hustle, fear, performance? Or are you multiplying truth, kindness, steady, identity-rooted light? This is where legacy begins—not in spotlighted milestones, but in small, ordinary, sacred moments: Stopping to ask someone how they're *really* doing. Confessing that you once froze, that you made a mistake—and what you learned from it. Choosing to be fully present with your kids, your friends, your team—when it would be easier to hide behind busyness.

The fear-driven achiever shows up in all of us. Sometimes he hustles for approval. Sometimes she hides behind control. Sometimes it's a limp you deny. Or armor you wear to look strong. Or power you cling to so you don't have to feel. Or silence you keep because desire feels too dangerous to name. But then comes a moment—a *now* moment—when the light is too clear to keep pretending.

Jacob limped into the sunrise carrying a name he didn't earn—but one he finally received. He had spent a lifetime grasping, deceiving, striving to prove himself worthy of blessing. But in the light, he stopped running. And the man who once schemed for identity became the father of a nation. The ripple was never just about his limp—it was about the people who would walk in the name *Israel*.

David stood on the battlefield, face to face with a giant who mocked him, dismissed him, labeled him small. It wasn't so different from today's branding—just louder and more raw. The fear-driven achiever might have flinched. But David didn't argue with the label. He picked up five smooth stones and answered it with action. Generations later, people still remember—not just the victory, but the *clarity* of that moment.

The ripple outlasted the roar.

Joseph had every reason to hide behind his success. He had power. He had position. He had survived betrayal, injustice, false accusation. The fear-driven achiever would've let the dream do the talking. But Joseph chose something different. When the brothers who hurt him stood before him, he broke. He wept. He forgave. And in that *now* moment, the pit no longer defined him. The grace did. His ripple wasn't power—it was restoration. Vision for a people who would've perished without him.

D.L. Moody once feared dying an ordinary man—unseen, unknown, unworthy of God's notice. But standing on a Chicago street corner, something shifted. He didn't make a boast. He made a vow: "By God's help, I will be that man." And he was—not because he proved himself, but because he surrendered. His ripple still fuels movements and missions today. Men and women still speak with fire born of humility because Moody chose light over fear.

And me? I wore my fear-driven achiever badge like armor—quiet, composed, intelligent, capable—until the pain caught up with me and dropped me. The hip injury didn't just break my stride. It broke the story I'd been telling myself—that strength meant staying in control. But in the recovery, something else surfaced: stillness, honesty, and the realization that I didn't need to hustle for worth anymore.

That being was enough.

That healing—when shared—
could ripple farther than any achievement ever would.

These are the moments when the light comes on. Not to shame, but to clarify. Not to destroy, but to free. The fear-driven achiever always wants to wait until it's safe. But legacy doesn't begin with safety. It begins with light. With clarity. With a single moment when you realize: I can't live like that anymore. And that's where the ripple begins. So I ask: What light have you been given that you're now responsible to carry? Where in your life, leadership, or relationships has clarity come that you can no longer ignore? And what ripple might begin the moment you stop waiting—and start living from it?

SHARED FIRE: WHEN SCARS BECOME SPARKS

Some wounds heal quietly. Others leave marks that never quite fade. I used to resent my scars—especially the ones I couldn't hide. The surgical lines across my hip weren't just physical reminders of pain. They felt like proof I'd fallen behind. Like visible evidence that the fear-driven achiever had finally lost the race. The verdict felt final: case closed.

But something shifted. Not all at once. Not in a grand, cinematic moment. But gradually. In conversations. In unexpected pauses. In the quiet look someone gave when I mentioned surgery… or the limp… or the season I disappeared to recover. People didn't recoil from the story. They leaned in.

It turns out, scars don't scare people. Pretending not to have them does. We've been conditioned to present our best angles. To be Instagram-ready. To lead from strength. To curate our narrative until it gleams.

THE RIPPLE EFFECT – WHEN YOU MULTIPLY THE SHIFT

But real connection doesn't happen when we impress. It happens when we bleed a little. When we say *me too*. When we choose presence over performance.

That's what fire does—it spreads. Not through shouting. But through sharing. Not through power. But through presence. Fire multiplies through honesty. Scars become sparks. And one act of truth can light a thousand unseen candles.

A few months after my second surgery, I had a chance to speak to a large group. I wasn't fully healed. I wasn't fully ready. I still moved slowly and carefully. My strength hadn't fully returned. But something deeper had—clarity. So I spoke.

For 30 minutes, I told the truth. My story. My background. My why. The collapse in the dark. The rescue. The ache of not knowing if I'd ever walk the same. The recovery—not just of my hip, but of my identity.

Afterward, there was applause. But inside, I panicked.

What have I done?
Will they see me differently now?
Did it even matter?

And then he stepped forward… A man, slightly older than me. "Thank you," he said. He had served in the U.S. Air Force. Injured his back. Put off getting help for years. Kept pushing through the pain. Doubling down. Powering forward.

But after hearing my story? "I'm going to make the call," he said. "I'm going to stop waiting." It was his inflection point. The light had come. He couldn't keep acting like he used to.

Behind him came another—a woman. Quiet. Vulnerable. Also nursing a hip injury. "I needed this," she said. "I'm going to get mine checked out, too."

As I packed up my things, more people approached. A hand on my shoulder. A quiet look of recognition. The kind that doesn't need words to say: I heard you. I carry that too. They had seen what honesty looks like in the light.

My story is expensive. It cost me more than a decade—physically, emotionally, internally, financially. But the ripple? The ripple is free. You just need someone willing to strike the match.

So I wonder—What has your story cost you? And are you still hiding it behind the façade of perfection, performance, or polish? Because your scars might just be the spark.

And the fire you carry? It's not meant to be admired. It's meant to be shared. To create light for others when they have none. When you tell the truth before you're fully healed, you give someone else permission to begin. That's legacy. That's fire. That's how the false identity begins to burn away—the one created by the fear-driven achiever. The mask. The image. The illusion. And that's how the ripple begins to multiply.

The ripple didn't start on a stage. It started with a scar. With a limp. With a quiet *me too* in a conversation no one recorded. That's the secret fear never tells you: that the smallest act of courage can become someone else's lifeline. That vulnerability travels faster than volume. And that real legacy never needed a spotlight—never needed a viral reel or a trending name.

THE RIPPLE EFFECT – WHEN YOU MULTIPLY THE SHIFT

We think impact is about visibility. But more often than not… It's about proximity. The fire that sparks something in someone else rarely comes from performance. It comes from presence.

THE RIPPLE MULTIPLIED: THROUGH PEOPLE, NOT PLATFORMS

That's the kind of fire that spreads. Not the loud kind. The lasting kind. Not a blaze fueled by performance. But a spark passed through presence.

But just as the fire begins to catch, the giants return. They shift their form. No longer shouting. Now whispering. In numbers. In metrics. In followers, reach, influence. In view counts, likes, applause. They say: the ripple must be *seen* to matter. They lie.

The giants are still talking. They just sound different now. They don't show up like warriors. They show up like algorithms. They whisper: your worth is found in being noticed. Influence is only real if it scales. Your story only matters if it goes viral.

But here's the truth: the ripple that matters most is often the one you'll never see reach the shore. Your giant wants you to chase visibility. Your purpose calls you to remain faithful. And the people who shape us most? They rarely stand on platforms. They walk behind us. They see what others overlook. They speak truth—quietly. In kitchens. In waiting rooms. On sidewalks. During long drives home. They don't chase influence. They multiply presence. And somehow—without a spotlight or a following—they change everything.

Legacy travels through people.
Not polish. Not performance. Not perfection.
People.

But this is where we get confused. We think *calling* is the measure of impact. What we do. Where we lead. What others notice. But calling is seasonal. It shifts with assignments, platforms, or titles.

Purpose, on the other hand, is permanent. It's not a job description. It's not a position. It's not a stage. It's a design. Wired into your being from the beginning—to create, to cultivate, to multiply life, light, and truth wherever you go. You don't have to earn it. You just have to live it.

Calling may be public or private, visible or hidden. But purpose is always present. And purpose always ripples. The fear-driven achiever chases calling to protect their identity. But when the calling fades, the fear returns. That's how the giant wins. But you weren't created to perform for applause. You were created to release what's in your hand. To live from your true name. To multiply truth and light into the lives around you.

The ripple doesn't start on a stage. It starts on the shoreline. Not with a spotlight—but with a scar. Not with certainty—but with surrender. You stood where the water met the land. Holding your story in your hands. And you let it go. That's all a ripple needs. Not performance. Not perfection. Just a person willing to break the surface.

The rock never sees the ripple. It just leaves your hand. It breaks the surface tension. Disturbs the quiet. Moves the molecules. Then disappears from view.

The water stirs. The clarity fades. But the motion begins. That's what truth does. It doesn't always look like clarity. It often looks like disruption. But movement is happening. Healing is spreading. Legacy is multiplying.

You don't need a stage. You need a shoreline—and the courage to throw what you've been carrying. The ripple is not your responsibility. The release is. So ask yourself: what story, truth, or scar are you still holding in your hand? What would it look like to release it? Not to go viral. But to begin a ripple.

THE FINAL WHISPER: WHAT NAME WILL THEY HEAR IN YOU?

D.L. Moody once said, "My greatest fear is not failure, but of succeeding at something that doesn't really matter." At the beginning of this journey, that quote felt like a warning. Now it feels more like a mirror—and a choice.

You've done the hard work. You've faced the giants. You've let the rock go. You've watched the ripple begin.

But the most powerful shift? You dropped the name fear gave you. You stopped striving to prove. You stopped curating an image. You stopped chasing applause. And now the whisper that moves through your life—it sounds different.

It doesn't say achiever. It doesn't say quiet one. It doesn't say not enough. It speaks the name you were meant to carry:
    Catalyst.
    Cultivator.
    Truth-bringer.
    Free one.

See, fear never needed you to fail. It only needed you to succeed at the wrong things. To win the wrong race. To build the wrong kingdom. To wear the wrong name. To stay stuck in a cycle that looked like success—but cost you your soul.

> But you've chosen a different path.
> You've chosen presence over platform.
> Purpose over performance.
> Legacy over likes.
> Release over reputation.

And that—that's what truly matters.

Here's the beauty of it all: You don't need to be fearless to live this way. You just need to stop obeying fear. Stop listening to the lies of the giant. You are not too old. You are not too late. You are not too broken. You are still echoing.

Maybe no one's applauding. Maybe your name isn't trending. Maybe you've stopped being the loudest person in the room. But someone is watching how you walk through pain. Someone is learning from your honesty. Someone is being freed by your courage to stop performing. Someone is seeing your scars and realizing they can heal too.

That's what an echo is. It's not a headline. It's not a platform. It's not applause. It's truth that keeps moving—even after you've stopped speaking. So yes…you are still echoing.

So ask yourself now—not what will they remember you for, but: what will they hear in you? Because every life whispers something. Not always in words. Sometimes in presence. Sometimes in scars. Sometimes in sacred silence or quiet wisdom. But it whispers.

THE RIPPLE EFFECT – WHEN YOU MULTIPLY THE SHIFT

The ripple has already begun.
The rock is gone.
The surface has broken.
The water is moving.

So now—what name will ride the wave?
What truth will echo from your life?

Because yes, the giants are still lying.
But your story?
Your story is still speaking.
And now… You know the difference.

So go ahead.

Let them hear your name.
Let them feel your fire.
Let them see your light.

Live what matters.

Am I Missing Something?

You've made it to the final chapter. You've done the hard work. You've seen what was hidden. And now… there's no going back. But still—something lingers. A subtle ache. Like the transformation isn't quite complete.

That's not the fear-driven achiever creeping back in. You are discerning correctly — there's a gap. Many fear-driven achievers experience a powerful shift when they finally name the giant and receive a new name — not the one fear gave them. But even after the lies go quiet, a strange silence remains.

The familiar rhythm of proving and pushing is gone. And in its place? A void. Left unfilled, that silence will draw many right back into old cycles—habits they thought were gone for good. But that is **not** your story.

So what fills the gap when the giant's voice finally goes silent?

Jesus.

This is your choice. Your moment. Like the story I shared from that junior high dance—Jesus is extending His hand to you. You don't have to earn it. You don't have to prove anything. You just have to say *yes*.

Step forward. Take His hand. Shut out the giant that's been lying to you. Because the truth is: **Greater is He who is in you than he who is in the world.** That giant cannot stand!

Jesus died for you—shedding His blood on the cross so you could be redeemed from the curse of sin and walk in freedom. Not just someday. Right now.

And if you're hearing a whisper that says:
"You don't need this."
"This is just religious talk."
"You're fine on your own."
"That prayer isn't for someone like you."

Don't believe it. That's the giant speaking again. Trying one last time to keep you from the truth. Had it not been for Jesus, I wouldn't be here. There was a moment—dark, quiet, hopeless—where the whispers nearly won. Where I believed I had no future, no purpose, no way forward if I couldn't walk.

But Jesus stepped in. With nail-scarred hands and light strong enough to pierce even that night. He met me there. And I lived. So can you.

PRAY THIS WITH ME

Dear Jesus,
I know that I am a sinner.
I ask for Your forgiveness.
I believe You died for my sins and
rose from the dead.
I turn from my sins and
invite You into my heart and life.
I choose to trust and follow You as
my Lord and Savior.
In Your name, Jesus, I pray and thank You.
Amen.

YOU ARE FOREVER FREE

You are free. You are whole. You are no longer defined by fear. You don't just have partial victory—you have complete victory in Jesus over the fear-driven achiever mindset.

So... what now?

THE JOURNEY FORWARD

Like any relationship, knowing someone requires spending time with them. And the good news? We have His Word—spoken and written—in the Bible.

Start reading it. Keep reading until it starts to read *you*. Until you hear the heart of Jesus speak back. You'll find truths that have echoed since the beginning of creation—that we were *blessed* from the beginning. Given grounded purpose. Meant to walk in it even now. Write down what speaks to you. Let it guide your steps.

Pray. Not just when it's hard—but all throughout the day. It's a relationship. Keep the conversation going.

Find a local church—surround yourself with others who live from the name Jesus gave them. Just like you now do.

Because the name Jesus gives you?

It cannot be taken away.

THIS IS THE MOMENT

You've dropped the old name—
The one fear curated for you.

Now live from the new one.

Out loud.
On purpose.
With urgency.

The giants are still lying.
But now…
you know the truth.

Go forward in freedom.
Go forth with the *real* truth.

Others need to hear what you now know.

This is your story now.

Let's begin.

WANT TO GO DEEPER?

If this book stirred something in you and you'd like to keep reflecting, I've created a free set of expanded journal prompts—organized by chapter—to help you continue the journey. You can access them anytime at:

oneJSPH.com

If you'd like to **connect** personally, **share** your story, or **learn** more about JSPH, feel free to reach out.

Email **info@onejsph.com**

You're not meant to walk this alone.

There is gold and a multitude of rubies,
But the lips of *knowledge* are a precious jewel.

Proverbs 20:15 NKJV

KEEP THE RIPPLE MOVING

Every story that breaks fear's hold creates a ripple.
And now, your ripple begins here.

The New Name Collective is a community where courage grows in connection — a place for readers, leaders, and creators who are learning to live from their true name, not the one fear gave them.

Inside you'll find transformational resources, devotionals, reflections, and conversations that keep this work alive — helping you walk it out long after the page closes.

Scan to Join *The New Name Collective* or visit **onejsph.com/collective**

Your story still moves the water — and someone else's courage begins with your ripple.

ABOUT RYAN

Ryan Finkle is a writer, speaker, and former fear-driven achiever who now helps others break free from the hustle to live from their true name. Blending biblical wisdom, personal story, and identity-centered coaching, Ryan speaks to leaders, creatives, and anyone tired of chasing worth through performance. His work invites readers into courageous presence, quiet legacy, and a life that echoes beyond the stage.

He doesn't write to impress.
He writes to remind you:

You're not too late.
You're not too broken.

And your story still matters

www.ingramcontent.com/pod-product-compliance
Lightning Source LLC
Chambersburg PA
CBHW070535090426
42735CB00013B/2990